MIGRATION TO MALDON

**THE STORY OF THE EVACUEES AND OTHERS WHO
CAME TO MALDON DISTRICT DURING WORLD WAR II**

Edited by

MARGARET ROOKE-MATTHEWS

.DEDICATION.

Thank you to all the people who contributed their memories to this book and entrusted me with their treasured documents and photographs to reproduce. This book is dedicated to you and all the other "migrants" who came to Maldon District during World War II.

.ACKNOWLEDGEMENTS.

Photographs, where indicated, are reproduced with the kind permission of the Imperial War Museum, London.

Pages from the Roll of Householders and Register of Accommodation, (reference: A9032 – 2 of 5 & 3 of 5 – D/B3, Montrose Road) are reproduced with the kind permission of Essex Records Office, Chelmsford, Essex.

Extracts from the Essex Chronicle from 1939, 1940 and 1942 are reproduced with the kind permission of the Essex Chronicle Series, Chelmsford, Essex.

King George's certificate to school children is reproduced with the kind permission of Councillor Frank Delderfield, of Maldon District Council, who was presented with the certificate in June 1946.

Photograph of Beeleigh Abbey reproduced with the kind permission of photographer, Den Phillips, Maldon, Essex.

Thanks to Henry Mason for initial proof reading; to Heather Gates who typed up the mounds of letters and interviews; to Justine Murphy who undertook all the research into how to publish and distribute the book; and to David Rust other staff at Maldon District Council who helped. Thanks also go to Jeremy Saltmarsh for help and support thoughout the project.

This book is not intended as a definitive historical document. These are people's memories, as written or dictated to the editor. Maldon District Council cannot take any responsibility for the accuracy of any of the information contained in this book.

Published on behalf of Maldon District Council in 1995 to commemorate
the 50th anniversary of the end of World War II.
Researched and edited by Margaret Rooke - Matthews
Design by Lisa Franklin of Design in Mind
Typeset by Stylize
Printed by Mayland Graphics

**Published in 1995 © Maldon District Council
ISBN 0 9526387 0 3**

CONTENTS

·INTRODUCTION·

SECTION I – THE EVACUEES

SECTION II – OTHER MALDON MIGRANTS

SECTION III – MALDON DISTRICT RESIDENTS

POSTSCRIPT

APPENDIX AND MAPS

INTRODUCTION

On 1st September 1939 a mass exodus started all over Britain as millions of children and other vulnerable people, such as expectant mothers, were moved from areas of risk to relative safety in the country. Many thousands were sent to stay in Essex. Of those thousands, several hundred arrived in the Maldon District for a brief stay; leaving memories which remained with both evacuees and residents for the rest of their lives.

To commemorate the 50th anniversary of the end of World War II, Maldon District Council commissioned this book to record the memories of the people who came to Maldon as evacuees. The project started as a small one, but grew and grew as dozens of people came forward with their reminiscences after an appeal for information went into the national press, regional papers and magazines.

Not only former evacuees contacted me with their stories. The foster parents who took them in, the teachers who taught them and other residents of the district all had their stories to tell. Letters also came from some of the "Land Girls" in the Women's Land Army, who were posted to the district to work on the farms, from women in the Services, and others who came to stay or visit during the war for a host of different reasons.

From the original idea of a small booklet about evacuees, with maybe a dozen contributors, the book "Migration to Maldon" was born. The following pages are compiled from the personal memories of over 60 people. They are either quoted straight from their letters or were interviewed by telephone or in person during early 1995. Some people were sent a list of questions which they used as the basis for their text.

When reading the book please remember that these are very personal stories, recalled after nearly 56 years by people who were very young at the time. It is not intended as a definitive historical record but more a flavour of a period in time which had a lasting and meaningful effect on all the people involved. Memory plays tricks over the years, so some of the memories recorded here do conflict and may not be quite accurate. In fact, two members from the same family disagree about the way they travelled to the district all those years ago. But that is part of the charm and fascination of recording oral history in this way. I have occasionally added a few notes in brackets to clarify the text and have edited a few of the stories for the sake of space, consistency or diplomacy. Other than these small editorial tamperings all the following stories are written by the people in their own words.

Some of the memories are sad, many are happy; all of them are moving. They are a testimony to the people of the Maldon District who took the youngsters into their homes and into their hearts. I hope you enjoy the book.

Margaret Rooke - Matthews
MALDON DISTRICT COUNCIL

Mothers watch from behind the barriers as their children leave a London station under the evacuation scheme.

Photograph – Imperial War Museum

"Right round the coast the beaches were wired off and some were mined."
Alice Rice

Photograph – Imperial War Museum – coastal town in 1940

SECTION I

·<>·

THE EVACUEES

·MAKING PREPARATIONS·

Early in 1939, when it seemed that war would be inevitable, an Emergency Census was carried out in the Borough of Maldon to find out how many households would be able to take in evacuees and homeless people. Every household in the district was required to fill in the Census Return. The census looked at who lived in each property, how many rooms it had, and the numbers of spare mattresses, blankets and sheets available.

It was found that in the district there were 12,364 habitable rooms (excluding sculleries, boxrooms and bathrooms), 804 spare mattresses and 1,464 spare blankets. Residents were also able to provide 1,805 clean sheets, which could be used as bandages in an emergency. Taking into account the 8,586 people normally resident, the compilers decided that there would be spaces for 5,177 people housed in temporary accommodation, of which 2,445 could be compulsory and the remainder voluntary.

The Roll of Householders, which is obtainable through the Essex Records Office, lists each household, records the information from the census and lists how many evacuees each house could be expected to take. The roll was updated on several occasions during the war, noting which houses had been destroyed by enemy action.

A second register contains the Billeting Payment Check Record. This register shows exactly which evacuee stayed in which house and lists the amount of fees paid to the foster parents. Although the register gives a weekly account of fees collected, it is not in all cases an accurate record of how long each child stayed in the district, as some foster parents did not collect the payments. The register shows the fixed fees for taking in evacuees. The fee for unaccompanied children was 10 shillings and sixpence per week for the first child, (52p in decimal coinage) and eight shillings and sixpence for each additional child (42p). People taking in adult evacuees received five shillings per week (25p) and each child who was not boarded (i.e. was being looked after by an accompanying adult) generated a fee of three shillings (15p).

Borough of Maldon.

Town Hall,

Maldon.

TELEPHONE:
MALDON ██.325 (2 LINES).

To the Householder or Occupier.

An Emergency Committee has been set up to deal with the problems which are likely to arise if an invasion of this Country is attempted, and to assist in the preparatory and exploratory work you are hereby required to complete this Return.

Address ....

Name of Householder ....

1. NUMBER OF PERSONS ORDINARILY RESIDENT.

    (a) Able bodied MEN between the ages of 16 and 65. ·... _____

    (b) Able bodied WOMEN between the ages of 16 and 65. ... _____

    (c) Able bodied men and women over 65. .... _____

    (d) Men and women physically unfit. .... _____

    (e) Children under 16. .... _____

2. Number of habitable rooms .... _____
    (Excluding scullery, and bathroom.)

3. Number of homeless people who could be accommodated
    temporarily. .... _____

4. How many mattresses and blankets can you) Mattresses. ... _____
    provide in an emergency for wounded, or)
    persons whose homes have been destroyed?) Blankets. ... _____

5. How many clean sheets can you give for bandages
    in an emergency. .... _____

NOTE. Under the Defence Regulations the Occupier of any premises is
    required by law
    (a) to furnish true information with respect to the accommodation
        contained, and to the persons living therein, and
    (b) to provide accommodation for all persons who may be assigned
        thereto. ·

Borough of Maldon Census Form

Essex Records Office

Borough of Maldon.
Emergency Committee
CENSUS RETURN

1. Number of Persons ordinarily Resident.
   (a) Able bodied men between
       16,and 65 years of age.   <u>2188.</u>
   (b) Able bodied women between
       16,and 65 years of age.   <u>3011.</u>
   (c) Able bodied men and
       women over 65 years.   <u>508.</u>
   (d) Men and women physically
              unfit.   <u>914.</u>
   (e) Children under 16 years.   <u>1965.</u>
                       TOTAL   <u>8586.</u>

2. Number of habitable rooms.
      (excluding scullery,boxroom,
         and bathroom)   <u>12364.</u>

3. Number of homeless people who could
   be accommodated temporarily.
               Voluntary.   <u>2732.</u>
               Compulsary.   <u>2445.</u>
                  TOTAL   <u>5177.</u>

4. Number of mattresses and
   blankets that can be pro-Mattresses. <u>804.</u>
   vided in emergency for
   wounded or homeless.   Blankets.   <u>1464.</u>

5. Number of clean sheets that will
   be given for bandages in an emergency.   <u>1805.</u>

A copy of the Emergency Committee Census Return

Essex Records Office

THE EXODUS STARTS

When the time came for the evacuation, the numbers who were actually allocated to the district were hundreds rather than thousands, probably to the great relief of the authorities. A few of these came as part of the mass exodus on 1st September 1939, two days before war was declared. However, most of them arrived on 3rd September; with Neville Chamberlain making his famous speech announcing the declaration of war as they travelled down. Some arrived later because they were on holiday at the time or were evacuated to other districts first. Others came as private evacuees – staying with relatives who already lived in the area, or in rented properties with their families – rather than being sent as part of a large school group. Although most of the people who responded to my appeal were evacuated as children, I did hear from two young mothers. One, who was evacuated as an expectant mother and the other, the wife of a school teacher who was evacuated with his school.

The vast majority of the children who were evacuated to the district came from Wanstead and Woodford on the London/Essex boarders. Schools included many of the junior schools in Woodford, Woodford Bridge, Woodford Green and South Woodford. As the response to my appeal came in, two schools were mentioned again and again – Wanstead County High School and Churchfields Junior School in South Woodford. (This was particularly fascinating for me as I grew up in South Woodford and attended Churchfields School myself in the 60s.)

Whole schools were evacuated together, gathering in their school halls to be ferried to a "secret" destination. Most of the children had never even heard of Maldon so they wouldn't have known where they were going even if they had been told! Feelings were a mixture of fear and excitement. They travelled by bus or train and several people remember a convoy of red London buses. They wore the obligatory name tag and each of them carried a bag with their clothes, their gas mask, and a ration bag with food for one day. Many people mention that the rations included a bar of chocolate and a can of corned beef. In most cases you can be sure that the bar of chocolate was finished by the end of the journey!

There are different stories about what happened when the children arrived. Some remember being taken to village halls, school halls or even the council offices, where they were allocated to foster parents. Others remember being delivered to the front doors of their billets. Either way it seems that the billeting was orderly and well organised compared to the memories recorded elsewhere of a sort of "cattle market" where children were lined up and chosen. In most cases it seems that the evacuees were pre-allocated to families; although from some of the memories I recorded it seems that in some cases the final decision was open to negotiation.

The children were mostly sent to homes in Maldon and Heybridge but some went to Wickham Bishops, Goldhanger and other parts of the district.

Some families only took one child to stay with them and others took in as many as three or four. Larger families were mostly split up and had to stay with separate foster parents.

Many people think of the inner city children when they think of evacuees, and there are stories elsewhere of evacuees who had never seen a cow or green field and couldn't cope with the culture shock of country life. Possibly some people in the district had a preconceived idea of London children and awaited their arrival with trepidation. However, the reality, in Maldon's case, was very far from this image.

The district of Wanstead and Woodford was very rural at this time, and the main difference between the two districts was that Maldon had the added bonus of being near the sea. A lot of the children appear to have came from middle class families and were far from the image of "city urchins" which some people may have expected. They lived in modern homes, with "proper" bathrooms and inside, flushing toilets (which was not always the case in Maldon District at the time!)

Perhaps because the children's lifestyle at home was not that dissimilar to what they found in their foster homes, most settled in very quickly. A few were moved on to a new billet because of a mismatch, and some were desperately homesick and went home within days. By the middle of September most of the children were settled in and, having enjoyed a few days holiday in their new town, it was time to go back to school.

DISTRICT *ACACIA DRIVE*

Ref. Nos. of Visitor's Book	Name and Address of Householder		Number of Persons Ordinarily Resident						Number of Habitable Rooms		Total			No. of Mattresses	No. of Blankets		Bedrooms Req. M. B.
			A.	B.	C.	D.	E.	Total									
18.	MR L. G. CLARKE 1, Acacia Drive. (2)	3/3/44	1	1	0	0	1	3			4	0	1	1	2	2	
19.	MRS F. J. BROWN 3, Acacia Drive. (2)	3/3/44	0	1	0	1	0	2			4	2	–	1	2	1	
20.	M/S J COATES 5, Acacia Drive. (2)	3/3/44	1	1	0	1	1	2			5	0	3	2	1	2	
21.	MR A. W. JOSLIN 7, Acacia Drive. (2)	3/3/44	2	1	0	0	0	2			4	0	2	0	0	2	
22.	MR F. F. LEWIS 9, Acacia Drive (2)	3/3/44	1	1	0	0	0	2			3	2	–	0	2	2	
	~~"Hawthorns", Acacia Drive~~ MR J. H. SHACKLOCK 11. Acacia Drive. (2)	3/3/44	1	1	0	0	2	4			5	2	–	0	0	0	
	MR W. STRATFORD "West Mount" (2)	3/3/44	1	3	0	0	0	4			5	2		0	0	2	
			7	9	0	3	4	22			29	8	2	4	7	11	

NOTE.—Apart from the Householders Name and Address it will probably be convenient if [...]

It is suggested, only Seven Householders should be [...]

COPYRIGHT S.E.1S. SHAW & SONS LTD., FETTER LANE, E.C.4. S 301 (R)

BEDDING ISSUED			BEDDING RETURNS			NAMES OF EVACUEES BILLETED WITH NOMINAL ROLL REFERENCE		
H.	B.	O.	M.	B.	O.	NAMES AND REFERENCE	NAMES AND REFERENCE	NAMES AND REFERENCE

KEPT IN PENCIL SO AS TO FACILITATE ALTERATIONS.
CH PAGE.

Page from the Roll of Householders, which logs the findings of the Emergency Census. There is an entry for every house in the Borough of Maldon.

Essex Records Office

EVACUATION SCHEME.

...V —
...ILDREN — U.C.
...RDED ... — C.N.
.... — M.
.... — T.
.... — H.
.... — C.
.... — E.M.

BILLETING PA

*IN CASE THE DATES ARE INAP

	...HOLDER	ADDRESS	POST OFFICE	DATE OF BILLETING ORDER	
A 5/14.	Mrs. Filby.	70f, Mill Road		14/9/39.	M
				4/11/39.	
E 2/16.	Mrs. Good.	70b, Mill Road,		10/9/39.	
A 4/8.	Mr. C. Hodge,	70j. Mill Road,		14/9/39.	
A 5/18.				19/11/39.	
E 1/19.					
E 4/2	Mrs Galley,	70, Mill Road.		3/4/34.	
E 4/5					
3 12/3.				3/4/34.	
E 4/2					
3 12/3.					
A 4/5.	Mrs. E. M. Sargent;	78, Mill Road.		10/9/39.	
E 1/3.				28/10/39.	
E 365808. E 1/14.	Mrs. Smith,	78b, Mill Road,		11/9/40. 6/11/39.	
3 12/2.	Mrs. E. L. Coker,	80, Mill Road		3/9/	

OLD MALDON WARD

SUMMARY.

A
N
P
Q
R
S
T
U
V
W
X
Y
Z

ENT CHECK RECORD.

PARISH MILL ROAD

E THESE BLANK COLUMNS ARE PROVIDED SO THAT WEEK NUMBERS CAN BE INSERTED.

F EVACUEE	†CLASS OF EVACUEE AND WEEKLY RATE		TOTAL WEEKLY AMOUNT DUE TO HOUSEHOLDER			REMARKS (TRANSFERS TO NEW BILLETS, ETC.)	POST OFFICE RECEIPTS 1939			
							SEPT.	OCT.	NOV.
	C.	R.	£	s.	d.		3 10 17 24	1 8 15 22 29	5 12 19 26
-Jacobs	U.C.	8/6							
Priske	U.C.	8/6		14	-	Transferred to 15, Fitch's Crescent			
Jacobs	U.C.	10/6		10	6	Returned home. See previous page			
Chamberlain	U.C.	10/6		10	6				
ofman	U.C.	8/6							
illiams	U.C.	8/6		14	-				
ofman	U.C.	10/6				Returned home.			
illiams	U.C.	8/6		19	-	Returned home. See later entry.			
Potter	H	21/-							
B. Potter	H	21/-				Returned to Woof.			
tter	T	5/-	2	4	-				
Potter	H	21/-							
tter	T	5/-	1	6	-	See later entry. Transferred to 52a, Victoria Road.			
Sargent	U.C.	10/6		10	6	Returned home			
ennedy	U.C.	10/6		10	6	Transferred to 29, Mount Pleasant.			
Gridley	U.C.	8/6							
Gridley	U.C.	8/6		14	-	Re-evacuated.			
L. Eveling	M	5/-							
Eveling	C.N.	3/-							
el Eveling	C.N.	3/-		11	-				

THE CRISIS

EVACUATION TO BEGIN TO-DAY

"PURELY A PRECAUTIONARY MEASURE"

It was officially announced yesterday that the evacuation of school children is to begin to-day. The scheme will take several days to complete, and is being undertaken as a precautionary measure, " in view of the prolongation of the period of tension."

The Government feel assured that the attitude of quiet public confidence will continue.

This evacuation comprises Greater London, and will apply to the following boroughs in Essex: West Ham, East Ham, Walthamstow, Leyton, Ilford, and Barking; also to Dagenham and Thurrock.

Parents will be told where their children are when they reach their new homes. The cost of the journey will be paid by the Government.

People who do not wish their children to be evacuated are not to send them to school until they hear further.

The children evacuated will be taken by teachers to their new homes in super districts and received by people who have offered to take them and look after them.

Ordinary railway and road passenger services are likely to be reduced to enable them to assist in the evacuation, and unnecessary journeys should not be undertaken by the public.

HOW THEY WILL TRAVEL.

THE ESSEX CHRONICLE was informed at the offices of the Essex Education Committee yesterday that the first batches of children to be evacuated in the suburban areas will assemble at their schools this (Friday) morning at 9 o'clock, in charge of their head teachers. Each child will be numbered by a ticket, on which brief details will be written. The children, taking one day's rations with them, will travel by rail or motor coach to various destinations, already prescribed for them. The children will move in " evacuation parties," and not in their usual classes —this will enable the large and smaller children to be mixed together. Parents will not travel with the children, but as soon as the latter are settled in their new billets the parents will be immediately notified of their addresses. The children's own teachers will be attached to them as far as practicable. " The parties will be mainly distributed about the rural parts," it was stated, " and every step is being taken to ensure a happy reception for them."

Other persons to be evacuated will be expectant mothers, blind persons, and cripples. The total number of evacuees will be three millions.

It was emphasised in a Ministry of Health statement yesterday that the evacuation is purely a precautionary measure. " No one," says the official statement, " should conclude that this decision means that war is now regarded as inevitable."

It was originally felt in Government circles that evacuation might cause panic and misunderstanding among the people.

The Opposition made a strong case that it would have the contrary effect of producing calm and relief in the knowledge that should the blow fall, at least the children would be safe.

BUS AND RAIL.

Some revision of 'bus and rail services in suburban Essex is likely to be necessary to-day, in view of the evacuation plans. Last evening the authorities were working out arrangements that would result in the minimum inconvenience to the general public.

ESSEX EVACUATION SCENES

Thousands of children from the evacuation areas in West Ham, East Ham, Barking, Ilford, Dagenham, Walthamstow, Leyton, and Thurrock were moved on Friday, Saturday, and Sunday to safer places " somewhere in the country." Expectant mothers, blind persons, and cripples were also evacuated. At all the centres the arrangements worked with remarkable efficiency, transport being by rail, road, and boat. At Dagenham early on Friday morning the children assembled at the Ford Jetty from the various schools. At Halbutt Street Senior School, one of the largest schools in Dagenham, over a thousand children arrived, with their hand luggage and gas masks, accompanied in many cases by their parents. They were marshalled by the school staff, and at the top of Kent Avenue parents who accompanied them had to stop in order to avoid congestion at the final stages of their journey to the waterside. There the mothers said good-bye to their children and, although they had no idea how long it will be before they meet again, there were brave smiles and cheery farewells. The children were full of good spirits, and it was only when the boys and girls had finally disappeared from sight that many mothers broke into tears. Meanwhile, many mothers who had not registered their children for evacuation and now wished them to leave visited the Council Offices for information. A long queue was waiting on Friday morning outside the Health Department, where officials worked unceasingly, dealing with the inquiries.

A BRIEF BUT HAPPY STAY

The evacuees shared the schools with local children. This rather stretched the resources of the schools and in some cases this meant that one group had lessons in the morning while the other had lessons in the afternoon. Memories are a bit confused about this, but it seems that the mornings or afternoons which were not spent in lessons were spent doing other activities such as music, sports or organised walks. Some children may have seen this as "lessons" while others thought of it as "play".

Possibly because the majority of the children came from a district which was not too dissimilar, the children mixed in well with the locals. Several people, mostly boys, mention a bit of teasing going on from both sides, but on the whole, the evacuees' memories are a glowing testimony to the friendliness and kindness of the local people. Each evacuee has different memories of their stay according to their own experience, but some stories are repeated again and again:

Several mention an incident when the school was fired on by a German aeroplane, and one of the evacuees, a keen plane spotter, actually made a record of the type of plane. However, memories are confused about this, with pupils at both Maldon County Primary and Maldon Secondary School recalling the incident as occurring at their school. As the schools are located next to each other it could be that both schools were hit. It is also possible that each school was hit on a different occasion. Unfortunately the official records for the early part of the war – when most of the evacuees were in the district – are now lost, but the district's Civil Defence War Diary, August 1940 – May 1945, has the following entry:

DATE	CASUALTIES	REMARKS
11/1/43	Nil.	Slight damage by machine-gun fire in Maldon at Wantz Road Senior School, houses in Fambridge Road and Acacia Drive.

Many tell stories about playing in Promenade Park and on Hythe Quay, which are on the River Blackwater at Maldon. The boys particularly remember hunting for bullets in a range which was used for shooting practise somewhere along the promenade. Other frequently mentioned local beauty spots are Beeleigh Abbey, which is on the outskirts of Maldon and is now privately owned, and the ruins of St Giles Leper Hospital, which date from the 12th century.

Sadds timber yard is also remembered by a lot of the evacuees; many of whom were given a trip around the yard during their stay in the district. Sadds was a big employer at the time, owning a large area of land at Fullbridge by the River Blackwater – where the supermarket and industrial areas are today.

During the war the company built boats in addition to its usual activities. Sadds was taken over by Boulton and Paul in the 1970s and the Sadds side of the business was later sold off to Jewsons, who still trade from the same site today.

The walk to school up Market Hill is mentioned many times. Market Hill is a very steep hill which joins Maldon High Street at the top with Fullbridge at the bottom. The route from Heybridge to Maldon passed close to Maldon East Railway Station, through Fullbridge and up Market Hill. As the school bus was rather unreliable, many of the evacuees remember trudging up and down the hill several times a day with mixed feelings.

Hythe Quay as it is today, with boats moored along the "Prom".

Promenade Park today, with St Mary's Church

MOVING ON

Some of the children were very homesick and went home quite soon. As this was the period of the so called "phoney war", others went home for Christmas in December 1939 and didn't come back. The rest stayed for many months, until they were re-evacuated by the authorities.

In May 1940, with Holland and parts of Belgium and France under enemy occupation, the Government decided that the district was no longer safe for children as it was on the east coast. The district was declared an evacuation area and the evacuees who were still in the district were moved on, mostly to Wales and Gloucestershire. Others decided to return home to their parents at that time, to arrive shortly before the Blitz; but that is another story.

Maldon and the Blackwater Estuary were later revealed to have been marked on Hitler's maps as possible landing places in "Operation Sea Lion". Luckily the invasion never took place.

However short their stay, most have very fond memories of their time in Maldon. Looking back with the benefit of hindsight after 56 years, many say how difficult it must have been for the local people to have such an influx of strangers coming into their homes, but how they were made to feel welcome. Some kept in touch with their foster parents for many years after the war and came back to visit, bringing their own children to see where they had stayed.

Some say coming to Maldon changed their lives. One remembers being fascinated by the boats when he was here and bought one as soon as he could afford it when he grew up. Others came to live in the district in later years, and one or two, who came as private evacuees, never went home again.

The residents of the district seem to have been philosophical about the situation and just rolled up their sleeves and got on with everyday life. Their stories are included in the book in a later section.

WANSTEAD COUNTY HIGH SCHOOL

A fairly large group of pupils came from Wanstead County High School in Wanstead, London, with their teachers. The pupils shared the facilities at Maldon Grammar School; with one group using the premises in the mornings and the other in the afternoons. Unfortunately neither school has any records of the evacuees, but a letter written by one of the evacuees during the war suggests that as many as 350 pupils were sent away from Wanstead County High School. These are the stories from several of the pupils and the wife of one of the teachers, told in their own words.

"There were genuine feelings on both sides as evacuees said goodbye to foster parents and boarded the train."
Eric Piercy

Photograph – Imperial War Museum – East coast re-evacuation. June 1940.

"Even today a whiskery chin reminds ? of the mixture of excitement and despa ? as I kissed my father goodbye outside the school." Eric B Piercy

"Even today a whiskery chin reminds me of the mixture of excitement and despair as I kissed my father goodbye outside the school."

Letter from Eric B Piercy, Derby

It was not until October of 1939 that I came to join my own school, Wanstead County High School, which had been evacuated to Maldon at the outbreak of war. Owing to the way the initial evacuation had been organised by boroughs, I had been in Bedfordshire with Sir George Monoux Grammar School, the corresponding school in Walthamstow where my parents lived and where I had been brought up. As the youngest member of the family, at 14 years of age, I was the only one to be evacuated and even today a whiskery chin reminds me of the mixture of excitement and despair as I kissed my father goodbye outside the school, before we were marched off to the station, suitcases in hand, gas masks in their little boxes slung round our necks and big labels attached to our lapels stating who we were and where we had come from. Two days later, standing outside a little shop in the Bedfordshire village of Ampthill I heard that dramatic announcement by Mr Chamberlain broadcast over the radio, "I have to tell you that, since no such undertaking has been received......we are now at war with Germany". My childhood world fell apart in that instant but it was to be some months before the war caught up with us properly, much of that time I spent in Maldon.

I do not remember the main part of the journey to Maldon or even much of what happened on my arrival but I have a very clear image still of that little train which took me, all alone in the carriage, across the fields and marshes from Witham to Maldon. The train, two coaches and a tiny push/pull steam engine reminiscent of the one later recalled in the film 'The Titfield Thunderbolt' was, even then, a relic of an earlier age. The little Victorian coaches were not divided into compartments, like other trains I had been in, and had a clerestory and wrought iron brackets on which gas (or were they oil) lamps were hung. The lamps were not lit in the misty glow of an October afternoon. Although I had been to the Essex coast before (Southend and Clacton) I had never been to Maldon and I have never felt so far from home or lonely as on that journey from Witham.

I must have found my way to Church House because that was where the headmaster (Mr Joseph) and senior staff lived – a sort of residential staff room. At first I was very unhappy and homesick and did not settle at all. Billeted on a family who lived beyond the Promenade Park I could not re-establish the relationship with friends from Wanstead who were spread out all over Maldon and Heybridge. Compared with the compactness of a London suburb, or even that village in Bedfordshire, Maldon seemed to spread for miles and that quiet solitude of the marshes and salt flats, which I later grew to appreciate and love, to the 14 year old was nothing short of agoraphobic.

Elsewhere the war was beginning to happen and I remember listening avidly to the Six O'clock News on the Home Service as the story of the Battle of the

River Plate unfolded and the final scuttling of the Graf Spee. Finally it all got me down and in a state of some despair I got on my bike and cycled home to Walthamstow. By this time it was early December and in spite of my feelings (or perhaps because of them) I remember that ride home very well. There were great stacks of sugar beets, as tall as houses, in the fields just beyond the hedges waiting to be collected for processing in the factories. The Maldon area was one of the first to develop the sugar beet industry, there was an experimental station nearby. Do they still fertilise the fields with fish and leave it to rot on the surface? In the end I was persuaded to return and perhaps because I knew that I could get home if need be, I settled down very much better.

I am sure that the dear lady I was billeted on, a Mrs Freeman, had a lot to do with it. She and her husband lived with their son on Spital Road. Their garden backed onto the hospital grounds and I have an abiding memory of the clock on the hospital which struck the hours through the night, and until I got used to it, woke me every hour on the hour. If I remember correctly Mr Freeman was associated with the Methodist Church and may even have been the organist there, they certainly had an harmonium in the living room.

They kept chickens at the bottom of the garden and one day they killed one or two. One was hung on the back of the kitchen door for some days and come the weekend Mrs Freeman said, "Eric, get the coopy down and we'll pluck it and get it ready for the oven". As I took it down it let out a great crow as the air left in its lungs escaped. So did I as I dropped it on the floor to make my own escape. It was my first experience of killing for the table.

There were allotments where the car parks are now, behind the shops in the High Street. As we got towards the spring of 1940 I spent many an evening there with Mr Freeman as we prepared the ground for sowing and planting. People were out there till dark engaged in the, then, important activity of 'Digging for Victory'. As things worked out I never did get to sample those vegetables.

We shared the school buildings on Fambridge Road with Maldon Grammar School. They had it from 8.30am - 12.30pm and we had it in the afternoons from 1pm - 5pm. We had science on Saturday mornings in the other secondary school in Wantz Road, now part of the combined comprehensive school. So our mornings were spent in all sorts of organised activities and sports. In the summer term of 1939 we had had a big fund-raising event back in Wanstead to provide instruments for the school orchestra, adding woodwind and brass to the predominant strings. Those of us in the orchestra (I played the violin) met for three or four mornings a week in the Friends' Meeting House on Chapel Street. Under the direction of our music master, one 'Spud' Parker, we would scrape and blast away trying at least to finish together. Over the winter of 1939 we built up a very good orchestra and in the spring of 1940 we played the incidental music when the Staff Dramatic Society put on a performance of 'The Ghost Train', the result of their own winter activities. The event was attended by many of our local 'Mums and Dads' as well as some who visited from London for the occasion. In between our official orchestra rehearsals, at breaks in the morning sessions, the unofficial 'jazz ensemble' would rent the air around the Friends' Meeting House as we let fly with our latest creations. At least one member of that group, dear old Den Croker, became a professional musician in later life.

It was a very cold winter that first winter of the war and I can remember trudging through the snow down the High Street with Mrs Freeman to the cinema by the bus station to see the 'Wizard of Oz'. There was a report in the local paper that someone had skated on the canal all the way to Chelmsford except for one stretch along the way. That was the first time it had happened in 100 years. Ice-flows on the Blackwater rose and fell with the tide, great blocks of frozen sea water and snow as big as a garden. We would run out onto the blocks and see how far we could get. The smaller blocks dipped alarmingly as you got towards the edge, you had to be quick to jump onto the next without getting a boot full. Someone claimed to have walked right across to the Heybridge Basin from the promenade. Looking back on it, it was a very foolish thing to do. Perhaps it was low-tide at the time!

As the weather improved we would spend our evenings in the Promenade Park and also wandering the lanes. I do not remember any conflict between ourselves and the local young people, we seemed to accept one another in spite of the fact that we had usurped their schools. Beeleigh Abbey was a favourite spot, down by the lock on the canal. I was disappointed, when I tried to take my sons to see it as little boys in the 1970's, that we could not get down there. The neap tides brought further excitement as the water rose to the top of the promenade wall, lapping on the path, so that sitting on the seat at the end, we felt completely surrounded by water. Is the tulip tree still as resplendent outside the courthouse in Old London Road? It was the first liriodendron I had ever seen in flower and although I have seen many since, the one in Maldon stands out as being the best ever.

After the Netherlands were invaded in the late spring of 1940 and the war came very much closer to us, it was decided that the east coast was no place for evacuees, indeed it later became part of an exclusion zone. It was in late May or early June when the mass migration took place. There were genuine feelings on both sides as evacuees said goodbye to foster parents and boarded the train. This time it was a more familiar train than the one which had brought me to Maldon six months earlier. Armed with a great pack of salad sandwiches, prepared by Mrs Freeman, which lasted me the whole of the eight or nine hours journey to Gloucestershire, I saw Maldon disappear across those same marshes and fields. My class were sent to a, then, very remote village about 11 miles from Gloucester called Redmarley D'Abitot and a new chapter in the experience of this 'Eastender' had begun.

Later on I returned home after taking my School Certificate exam at Chippenham in Wiltshire, where the school finally settled down. I continued my education in Walthamstow until at 18 I was called up and started my Army Service at Warley Barracks near Brentwood, now the site of the Ford headquarters. I served for four and a quarter years with the Royal Corps of Signals, my war service taking me from Normandy to Berlin and then, when the war was over, I was sent to Greece, Egypt and Palestine. My wife and I have been to Maldon several times with our family over the years and it says something of my feelings for the town that at one time we did consider the possibilities of retiring there after I had finished my career in teaching. However, we had to let the idea go for various family reasons.

After 55 years I look back on my experiences in that part of Essex with its estuaries and salt flats, its birds and open windy expanses with pleasure and also those few months when I was an honorary Maldonite.

"I found myself in, to me, an unknown country town on the River Blackwater."

Letter from John H Cann, Leigh-on-Sea, Essex

In 1939 I was a 13 year old schoolboy living in Ilford and a pupil at Wanstead County High School. War broke out in the September of that year whilst I was on holiday staying at relations in Buckinghamshire. By the time I returned home my fellow schoolmates had already been evacuated by train to Ipswich and were to be subsequently re-located in Maldon. It was October before a billet became vacant and I found myself in, to me, an unknown country town on the River Blackwater.

I was billeted with a family named Bennett in Station Road, close by the side of the then Maldon East Railway Station. Station Road, apart from serving its obvious venue, was also the access to Sadds' timber yard. The husband of the family I stayed with was at that time a chauffeur to the Sadd management. Opposite the terrace I was billeted in were a number of wooden built cottages which backed on to the river. I can remember my hosts pointing out the discolouration on the walls where floods in earlier years had left their tidal-mark.

Our education was, of course, on a somewhat limited basis. We shared the Maldon Grammar School off the High Street with the local pupils. They attended in the mornings, we in the afternoons.

Mornings were occupied mainly with various forms of organised sports; from PT in a church hall off Market Hill (probably what is now the United Reform Church) to cross-country runs, inevitably through part of the muddy grounds of Beeleigh Abbey.

Weekends were generally free from organised school activities so we made our own amusements. My hosts had two sons a few years younger than myself and with them or my school friends we passed some happy hours walking or cycling (on a borrowed bike) round the nearby countryside. A favourite excursion was to Heybridge Basin, either along the road or the canal towpath. The promenade and the Hythe by the bath wall was a popular rendezvous.

The winter of 1939/40 produced some quite severe weather and at some time

I remember the river was frozen over from the road bridge to the railway viaduct that carried the branch-line to Maldon West Station. The ice was thick enough to skate on and a considerable number of people, myself included, enjoyed the sport.

Christmas came and we were allowed back home for the holiday. So it was off by train to Ilford for a fortnight, returning in the New Year.

This early period of World War II became known as the "phoney war" as very little hostile action took place. We did one night, however, have an air raid warning. There was no air raid shelter so we all huddled in the front room in our night-clothes. We were joined by an elderly couple from one of the timber cottages across the road, their home being considered a high fire risk. After a short interval the 'all-clear' sounded and we returned to bed. It later transpired that an unidentified aircraft had been sighted off Southend-on-Sea and the red-alert had been brought into action.

On another occasion I had gone to the cinema (it must have been a Saturday afternoon) when the power failed in the middle of the performance. I can remember the manager came onto the stage and amid catcalls from the audience announced that a barrage balloon had broken adrift from its moorings and trailed its cable through the overhead power-lines. The rest of the cinema show was cancelled. That was about the only hint of war we had at that time.

At Easter we were released home again as at Christmas and during that holiday I fell ill with chicken-pox. By the time I had recovered the school at Wanstead had re-opened on a part-time basis so I never returned to Maldon. In fact it would be 50 years before I set foot in the town again. The evacuated portion of the school later moved to Chippenham in Wiltshire whilst I and my fellow scholars in the London suburbs faced the 'Battle of Britain', 'The London Blitz' and the rest of the war. But that's another story.

My parents managed to visit me about every six weeks or so whilst I was at Maldon although travel was difficult. To most of us I think this period of our lives was just an adventurous adjunct to the normal. I felt occasional pangs of homesickness, but they were soon forgotten in the day-to-day activities. The people of Maldon were kind to us, though I never kept up contact with the people I stayed with. But that brief stay of six months will always be in my memory. Particularly tramping up and down Market Hill half-a-dozen times or more a day!

"Several of the men who kindly showed us round had one or two fingers missing. A by-product of the saw mills!"

Letter from Frank Edmonds, Islip, Northants

I noticed your letter in the spring edition of "Yours" and as one of those many children evacuated to Maldon perhaps the following may be of some interest.

When war broke out I was 14 years old and on holiday. On return to my home at Ilford, arrangements were made for me to be evacuated, and this was on a Borough Council basis. As such I was sent to Ipswich along with other children from Ilford. My school, Wanstead County High, was however evacuated to Maldon, and so after a fortnight arrangements were made for me to join my school mates and I was moved to Maldon. In this way I was not part of the "mass influx" of evacuees.

I was billeted with a very nice couple, a Mr and Mrs Lilley at "Crossways" Cross Road, which was a flat above the Co-op shop. Mr Lilley was the Co-op butcher. Not long after this I was joined by a colleague of mine, Henry Tanner and we both shared a double bed in the flat. At first there was no schooling, and we were free to roam about and explore Maldon, which we found most interesting. One day walking alongside the river, by one of the old boat sheds, I looked in and saw another of my school chums working on a naval whaler. I was invited in and was shown how to fit copper rivets into the planks of the clinker hull, using washers and a heavy dolly behind to absorb the blows of the hammer. This was very interesting and enjoyable, and I trust that my efforts were satisfactory as these boats were to be used as lifeboats in the war. I have returned to Maldon after several years to see the old boat yard, but there was very little going on then.

Opposite my billet a little way along the road was the distributing studio for the radio relay network which was fed all over Maldon on overhead cables and was a distinct feature of the town. So far as I can remember four stations were relayed. I have no doubt that this has long disappeared!

The winter of 1939-40 was one of the hardest on record at the time, and we had a severe cold spell. I found the river fascinating at this time. The tidal rise and fall must be at least 10 feet and of course of salt water, yet it froze over on each incoming tide, and when it ebbed the ice which was about two inches thick cracked and collapsed in almost vertical sheets, making it impossible to walk on. These edgewise sheets, stacked against each other, were added to by each fresh tide. As far as I remember there was still a navigable channel left in the centre of the river.

The snow fall was also very spectacular and a huge snow drift had built up on the inland side of the sea wall, in the hollow along the "front", (which had a fun fair in it during the summer months). This drift was all of 10 feet deep, and my pal and I were walking along on the promenade above the dip, and being young and full of beans, were enjoying the snow. I think he got too near the edge, and to my surprise, suddenly completely disappeared, and emerged at the bottom of the bank, none the worse for his trip!

When the warmer weather came quite a few of us school children enjoyed ourselves in the open air swimming pool on the riverside.

We finally went to school at the Maldon Grammar School, sharing the accommodation part time. I remember the school woodwork shop was down a little lane off the High Street, almost opposite the corner with Market Hill. I was very impressed with the local woodwork teacher and learnt a lot from him, which I have put to good use in later years. No doubt this workshop has also gone the way of so many things now!

In my mind I can see Market Hill very clearly with its 1 in 7 slope and sharp bend leading down to the railway station, river bridge, and Sadds' timber yard on the opposite bank. There were always many tree trunks floating in the water alongside the yard, which I understood was a way of seasoning the timber before sawing. On one occasion we were taken around the timber yard and one thing made quite an impression upon me.....several of the men who kindly showed us round had one or two fingers missing. A by-product of the saw mills!

Not too far away towards Heybridge Basin was a bridge over the canal and just below it we could hire out a rowing boat and enjoy an afternoon on the calm water which runs up to Chelmsford, (not that we went more than a few yards either way!)

Little did I know that my experiences in Maldon were to be a forerunner of designing and building my own fibreglass cruiser, (diesel engined with a 25ft x 6ft beam), and exploring many of England's 2000 miles of canals. When I retired I was lucky enough to get a house with a mooring at the bottom of the garden on the River Nene here in Northamptonshire.

In June 1940 it was decided that Maldon was perhaps not the safest place for children with the war developing as it did. As a result with the rest of my school we were taken to Newent in Gloucestershire and later to Chippenham in Wiltshire.

Over the years we have revisited Maldon several times and still enjoy the walk along the front with its bracing air, and the atmosphere of the old sailing barges moored upstream. As a member of my local Historical Society I wish now that I had been more attentive to the very attractive "old world" parts of the town, but I guess you can never have an old head on young shoulders!

"I remember a lady asking the billeting officer for two clean girls! Obviously boys from London were to be avoided."

Letter from David Freeman, South Woodford, London E18

I was due to start at Wanstead County High School in September 1939 but at 10.00am on Sunday morning the 3rd, I, with an older brother was put on a red London double decker bus outside Ray Lodge School, Woodford Bridge. We were off to Abridge someone whispered.

In fact it was Heybridge but the aspirate was dropped by the East Londoners.

We were debussed some two hours later at the corner of Crescent Road and Holloway Road in Heybridge, by which time we were at war. We stood with our labels round our necks and our belongings in a small attaché case waiting to be selected. I remember a lady asking the billeting officer for two clean girls! Obviously boys from London were to be avoided. At last as the numbers diminished we were taken in by a family from Holloway Road. It was a very long day for all of us but as a 10 year old I have no memories of homesickness or fear.

Our new home was truly a family home, full of interesting things and people. There was, I can remember, the biggest Meccano set I had ever seen and, in the garden in the course of construction, a 20' sailing boat. The yacht was launched on the Blackwater and sailed very well.

The family comprised of: father, who was employed in a senior capacity at Bentalls; mother, who had been a teacher; two grown-up sons and a daughter who was about four years older than me.

The winter was very severe with snowdrifts of six feet and more on the various country roads around Heybridge. The Moores buses (Bedfords) could not always run; so we walked to school. The Education Authorities discovered us after a short time at Heybridge Junior School and I was asked to join Wanstead County High School at Maldon Grammar School. Some of my fellow pupils were billeted in a large house/mill by the bridge over the Chelmer canal at the Heybridge end of the Causeway and we all walked to school from there.

We shared the day with Maldon Grammar School pupils; sport in the morning and lessons in the afternoon. If the weather was too inclement in the morning, we went to the Market Hall for organised singing. By Christmas a Nativity play had been organised and I was one of the three wise men.

We managed to get home for Christmas thanks to the son of our hostess who drove us in his Austin Seven to Chelmsford, where we continued our journey by train. Quite an exciting ride because of the ice and one of my first motor-car rides.

Unfortunately, although not aware of any change in my health, I became rundown and could not make it back to Maldon after the Christmas holiday. However, in 1940, Wanstead County High School opened at Wanstead with Ilford County High School and by mid-year I was off again with the school to Gloucester and then Wiltshire.

In hindsight I feel that although evacuation broke up many families, not all experiences were bad. We remained in touch with our "family" in Heybridge with visits and letters until both "parents" died.

My memories include "skating" on the canal and a slide on the frozen boating lake at Maldon and the enjoyment we got outside despite the weather of that bleak winter.

May I put on record my thanks to the people of Heybridge and Maldon who put up with us as did many more receiving centres around England at that time.

Further, I think it ought to be said that my family of mother, father and three boys, was never together again, apart from one short period when one brother was on embarkation leave for Japan with the Navy and as the other returned on disembarkation leave after four years in Africa (with the RAF), to mid-winter England in 1946. By the time I had returned from my National Service with the Army very nearly 10 years had passed!

"I wonder if all this would have happened if I had not taken my first national examinations at Maldon in 1939."

Compiled from letters from Miss Doreen M Hill, Southsea, Hants

I was 15 years old, living at Ilford, Essex, and about to start the new term in the 5th form at Wanstead County High School. When evacuation took place I told my parents that I did not want to leave my home and continue studying, although I loved school and had intended going eventually to University to study languages. I decided instead to find a job and start work.

The school had been evacuated to Maldon and my parents soon received a letter from Mr Joseph, the headmaster, pointing out that if I missed the opportunity to take the School Certificate Examination I would probably regret it later in life and he suggested that I should evacuate for a few months in order to sit the examination with the rest of the 'A' stream at Christmas. We had done well in the mock examinations in the summer and were expected to achieve good results.

Consequently I found myself being taken by some kind neighbours in their car to Maldon. No new billets were available but my friend Sheila Stack was lodged with a Mrs Seaman, who agreed to take me in. Her husband worked at the Co-op and they had a little girl of three called Molly Ann.

Our school shared the Maldon Grammar School with the local pupils and we had use of the premises in the mornings. I remember practice air raid warnings, when we all had to go and sit in the corridors and try to continue working there. On some afternoons Mr Joseph would take a small group of us to a house which he rented and give us extra tuition to help us prepare for the forthcoming examinations.

The weather was bitterly cold and although I worked hard I made up my mind to go home again as soon as the examination results came through in the New Year. I duly took the papers in English, mathematics, French, German, Latin and biology.

On Sundays I went to the local Wesleyan Methodist Church, having always attended our local Methodist Church at home. When I first made enquiries locally I was asked whether I was a "Prim" and was nonplussed, never having appreciated that the Methodists had split into Prims and Wesleyans. Weekday evenings and part of the weekends were spent doing homework, with some difficulty as little Molly Ann naturally expected us to play with her when we were home. Having no spare money there was no social life and we would wander in our spare time, getting colder as we got nearer to the water.

Mrs Seaman had agreed to take me until Christmas and when I returned after the holiday I was taken in by Mr and Mrs Raymond who lived in Heybridge. Mr Raymond was a carpenter and worked at Sadds. He was a great craftsman and I still possess a table lamp which he made for me when I left. The Raymonds had a daughter, Joyce, who was an apprentice hairdresser. She was only a year older than I was but seemed grown up to me and she had a boyfriend, Cyril. When Joyce came home from work on the day I arrived we had a somewhat stilted conversation until about nine o'clock, when I took myself off to bed. I did not put my school uniform on until the next day, and I learned later that when I had gone to bed Joyce asked her mother what had happened to the little evacuee they were expecting. My efforts to appear as grown up as she did had led her to think that I was one of the teachers. It did not take long for us to become good friends and I remember playing darts with her and Cyril and also getting up to mischief with apple pie beds, etc. We are still good friends and it was Joyce who sent me the newspaper cutting which led to these notes.

I loved staying with the Raymonds. Using the spotlessly clean outside toilet on a cold winter's night was quite an experience, as was listening to the "Nightsoil" men who came late at night twice a week to empty the pan. On bath night Mr Raymond would occupy himself somewhere, having put the tin bath in front of the fire for me and filled it with lovely hot water. Even the most modern bathrooms do not give me as much pleasure as the soaking I enjoyed by the fire as I performed my ablutions on cold winter days in early 1940. Mr Raymond also dug out an old bicycle for me to use on my weekly evening class visits to Maldon to study book-keeping. The oil lamp on the handlebar was filled for me before I set off in the darkness.

Those of us who had taken our School Certificate were now put in the 6th form, to give us a different experience and prepare us for the future. We received a request from the local council for volunteers to help in the Local Defence Office, in a clerical capacity, and I happily went along to do my bit. The gentleman in charge was a Colonel Cockburn, who seemed quite formidable to me at the time. For some reason I think of him now when I see repeats of "Dad's Army", with Mr Mainwaring.

I am afraid that I can remember very little of the actual work which I, with other 6th form volunteers, did at the Local Defence Office, as I was only there for a few weeks in early 1940 before returning home. There was talk of war and invasion by the Germans and our duties probably involved keeping records of plans for air raid precautions, dealing with casualties, etc., though nothing stands out in my mind after all these years.

Although I was not yet 16 I do remember that things seemed a bit chaotic – what my father would have called a "Fred Karno" outfit, and no-one really seemed to know quite what we would do if the Germans did arrive. Perhaps it is just as well that they did not strike in our direction at that time.

I returned home at the end of February. Some time later that year, my fellow evacuees were all moved to Chippenham in Wiltshire, which seemed a much more sensible idea, as Maldon would have soon been over-run, being so near the east coast.

I have never forgotten the great kindness shown to me in so many ways in my few short months at Maldon and Heybridge. The local people must have dreaded the invasion of so many young people almost as much as they later feared the expected invasion of the Germans, yet they opened their homes and hearts and made it possible for us to continue our lives with minimum disruption or distress. The head teachers and staff of local schools must have spent many wearisome hours working out timetables, and arranging lessons as well as billets for the newcomers, the authorities must have worked overtime for many weeks trying to produce order out of the chaos caused by the outbreak of war and disruption to families, travel and life in general, and the local population including children and teenagers showed enormous tolerance and forbearance. Those of us who were on the receiving end, whether little evacuees or tall teenagers like myself have cause to be grateful and thankful for all that was done for us at that time.

I went on to become an office clerk, then a shorthand typist, then a Wren, then a secretary in London, then to an Emergency Training College and later to the Sorbonne in Paris before becoming a teacher of French and English, eventually coming to Portsmouth as head teacher of a local secondary school. I wonder if all this would have happened if I had not taken my first national examinations at Maldon in 1939.

"It was quite a sight to see boys and masters vanishing as soon as they spotted him rounding the corner."

Letter from Mrs Molly Huxley, King's Sutton, Banbury

On a cold winter's evening, on November 10th 1939 I arrived at Maldon East Railway Station, having travelled all day by train from a suburb of Liverpool, with my new baby, now three and a half months old. My husband was there to meet me. He had been in Maldon since early September, when, as a young schoolmaster and teacher of French, he had accompanied a party of boys from Wanstead County High School. I had stayed behind at my parents' home to recover from the birth which had been long and hard.

Sid had secured a billet with Mr and Mrs Dykes of Wantz Chase, a bungalow. Paradoxically, they had sent their seven year old daughter Muriel away from the coast and we had moved in. There were two boys still at home, Arthur and 16 year old Derek. Although the latter was not at an age when a boy is most attractive, he belied such a judgement. He was not only good-looking, but was well-mannered and thoughtful and it saddened me greatly when, by falsifying his age, he got into the Army and was killed within the year.

There was also a sister, Connie, who was married and had a young baby, Pauline Ann Saunders, and when her husband went into the Army she moved in with her parents. The three of us, Connie (21), me (31) and Mrs Dykes (41) gossiped happily in the kitchen when the men were out.

Connie missed her husband very much and I can see her now, on her knees mopping up icy water that had flooded the passage after a pipe had burst, constantly moaning, "Wha' is my life?"

Mrs Dykes was unfailingly cheerful and kind (unlike some of the other hostesses we had later in other parts of the country) and more than tolerated my baby. She was also very scrupulous about keeping our rations in separate containers. Her husband was a tall handsome man who had been in the Guards; and as an only child had been thoroughly spoiled by his mother. She still kept a small general store at Fullbridge at the bottom of Market Hill. As one of his jobs was to drive the hearse he would go down to the shop in it each Friday morning to collect the week's takings. He would then return home for his mid-day meal, leaving the money on the seat. There was no danger of it being stolen. The people in Maldon were completely honest.

As the boys only had the use of the school in the afternoons, every morning they were at a loose end. Mr Joseph, their headmaster, tried to keep an eye on them by strolling down the High Street every morning. It was quite a sight to see boys and masters vanishing as soon as they spotted him rounding the corner. The boys would dive into the shops, while the masters, feeling a sudden thirst, would disappear into the Blue Boar – also a favourite resort in the evening. There they would be joined by the two women staff who had come with us – Miss Skittery and Miss Shurvy. As they were often together they were known collectively as Skit and Shurvy, (a trap for anyone given to Spoonerisms). The art master "Spud" Parker liked the company of the young masters in the Blue Boar in the evening regardless of "the little women", left behind in a dimly lit billet. This used to annoy some of us "little women" very much, as it never occurred to our husbands to disappoint "Spud", and we couldn't forgather as we had such small children and didn't want to impose on our hostesses to baby-sit.

We were later billeted at "Highlands" with Mrs Pirie, a surgeon. Her husband, also a doctor, was in the Army, her daughter, Mary, training as a doctor, and her son, John, away at Stowe School.

Mrs Pirie looked vague, but, in fact, missed nothing and was extremely precise. Breakfast was at 8.00am not one minute past. We were asked how many cups of tea we drank at breakfast and at tea-time, so that the exact number of cups of water (plus half-a-cup for evaporation) could be put into the kettle. The three lavatories in the house were allocated specifically. Woe betide anyone caught using the wrong one. I could sense that Mrs Pirie disliked the invasion of her home by evacuees, (a term which was now derogatory). However, she had a keen sense of duty and never failed to be courteous.

We were given her husband's study for a sitting room and there I spent my evenings alone, while my husband played his part in keeping depression away from the expounder of the art of drawing. I occupied my time reading the books on the shelves and acquired a smattering of useful medical knowledge.

Although I was quite busy looking after my baby, I felt that when the maid left, I ought to do a bit to help – washing dishes seemed the most obvious. Then when John came home for the Easter holidays with some maths to be done as a holiday task, and his mother thought he ought to have help with it, I offered my services (I had taught maths before marriage) so each morning when baby

Laura was settled outside in her pram, we used to sit down to work. Mrs Pirie was pleased when he scored the highest mark on his return to school, and, for me, it did a little towards wiping out some of the stigma of being a homeless evacuee.

The cold weather at long last gave way to spring and summer, and the tennis court came into use. We were allowed to use it so long as we kept the surface rolled. I had to buy myself a new tennis racket, at a shop in the High Street, not far from St Peter's Church, and in the window was a china breakfast set on a tray, and when I heard Mrs Pirie admire it I knew what to give her as a parting gift.

Carefully graded tennis parties were arranged. We were included with the school teachers, amongst whom was Mr Deedes, the grammar school headmaster – a very likeable man. When more elevated company was expected, I was relegated to making the coffee and my husband to bringing up the bottles from the cellar. "Your department, I think!" said Mrs Pirie. He was a bit taken aback, having always imagined that his destination in the evenings was a secret.

At the beginning of June we left Maldon and moved inland to Gloucestershire as there was a threat of invasion after the evacuation of Dunkirk.

You may wonder why my husband wasn't in the Army. He would love to have been, but was graded C3 because he was lame. He died of multiple sclerosis 30 years ago.

I have visited Maldon on rare occasions since. I think it is a beautiful little town – and so friendly. They must have hated having us invade their homes.

Some years after the war Mrs Pirie came to have lunch with us in Chelmsford, and her first remark was "I can see you don't like housework" – observant as ever!

"I'm very grateful to them for, among other things, teaching me to play solo whist."

Letter from Joyce Gooby (Née Cooke), Broadstairs, Kent

I was evacuated to Maldon with Wanstead County High School in October 1939, 12 years old, but we only stayed about six months before the school was moved to Hartbury – near Gloucester.

My "family" was Mr and Mrs Blowers in King Street, who were both members of the Salvation Army, and I'm very grateful to them for, among other things, teaching me to play solo whist, and allowing me to "sit in" when they had friends in to play (one was a Mrs Filby, who was landlady of a nearby pub).

They also had an extremely tame budgie who used to sit on your hands and try to take the cards.

Mr and Mrs Blowers had a married son who was also in the Salvation Army and was a bus driver (he also played a mandolin) and I think lived in Mount Pleasant.

I remember walking to Maldon Grammar School for lessons across some allotments, where Mr Blowers grew some sprouts when he discovered they were my favourite vegetable. It was a very bad winter and the allotments were covered in deep snow, resulting in many snowball fights on the way to and from school.

I also remember going to a church at the top of a hill and walking to Heybridge and Beeleigh Abbey. Also we used to go to the church hall to knit sea-boot stockings for the ships "adopted" by the school. Funny the things that stick in your mind in those unhappy times isn't it?

Everybody was very kind and I was very upset when we had to leave.

I am now 67 and a widow, with one son – one grandson seven years and identical twin granddaughters two years old!

"It seems very absurd that we should be evacuated then come back to London for weekends and holidays."

Letter from Mrs Beryl Thorn (Née Curnock), Saxmundham, Suffolk

Sunday September 3rd 1939 I was evacuated (in a London Transport red double decker bus) to Chelmsford. I was billeted with my friend Esme Cook in King Edward Avenue with Mr and Mrs Patrick – he worked in the accountants department in the offices of Essex County Council a few yards away at the end of the road. My general feeling is that we – Wanstead County High School, a co-ed school – were not welcomed by King Edward School where we reported occasionally (for air raid practises and no schooling!)

According to my letter of November 15th 1939, written to my pen friend in Australia, we were only in Chelmsford for two weeks. Hence we arrived on 17th September in Maldon. I seem to remember it was a Sunday. We travelled this time in Eastern National single decker green buses and were taken to Maldon Grammar School – a welcome here! – and where we were sorted indoors in the classrooms and allocated to our billets. (I seem to remember at Chelmsford walking with a billeting officer along the streets with a group of school mates and the officer knocking on the doors!)

Mr and Mrs Taylor, (he was East Maldon Railway Station Master) were both very kind and welcomed Esme and myself into their house. Their eldest son (or daughter?) was married and lived at Southminster and visited frequently. The next one in the family was in her 20's – she was always called Bill and lived at home – seemed to be very busy one way and another, but always had time for Esme and myself and I so much enjoyed the many walks that we had with her of a weekend along the river or canal. Joan, the youngest in the family was of similar age to Esme and myself (15 years) and she attended Maldon Grammar School – somehow we didn't seem to see so much of Joan – probably mainly due to the fact that she was off to school early in the morning and our times were completely different.

Our host school, Maldon Grammar School, I think started their school day at 8.30am and they had lessons until 1.00pm, with their afternoons free for games, etc. From 1.30pm Wanstead High School were given the use of the grammar school premises so we had lessons there from 1.30pm until about 4.30pm. Maldon Grammar School made us feel welcome.

Mrs Taylor fed us very well and every day she prepared a hot meal for all her family and for Esme and myself – serving it at 1.00pm – real country home cooking, and Yorkshire pudding as an accompaniment everyday apart from Fridays when we had fish! So Esme and I immediately after lunch struggled up Market Hill (our bikes accompanied us everywhere, and our families had brought them from home with them on an early visit by train to Station House – again Mr and Mrs Taylor were welcoming to our families).

Life at Station House of course revolved around Mr Taylor's duties as station master – no trains at all on a Sunday and I seem to remember realising how easy it was to push the turntable round!

My stay in Maldon is full of very happy memories – even with the pressure of School Certificate exams and constant homework and studying, there were many activities held in the various denominational church halls throughout the town during the morning – needlework (not my favourite) singing I particularly enjoyed and also I learned to play (or tried to play) the flute with a small orchestral group in the Friends' Meeting House. I loved exploring all the little side lanes and passages along by the river; I was fascinated with all the barges under sail along the river. We often played hockey on the fields beyond the church and were told of the battles fought there in Saxon times (though I presume that was really nearer to Osea Island and not near the church). The extra lessons that we had of a morning were held upstairs in the front room of the house where our headmaster Mr Joseph and his wife were living – the room was quite bare with no floor covering, just the floorboards and with trestle tables I think and chairs. The house was in a side road off the High Street.

In April 1940 Esme and myself moved billets as Mr and Mrs Taylor were having a holiday, and we lived then with a couple of the name Brown, I think, towards the further end and on the right of Fambridge Road. We were only there for just four weeks. Hitler had invaded Holland and Belgium and his Army was rapidly capturing countries across Europe: so it was imperative that we were moved together as a school to an unknown destination – it all happened on a Sunday – probably 19th May. We had to assemble at Maldon East Railway Station, early morning, when a steam train very soon arrived. Even Mr Taylor did not know where our destination would be apart from the short local line first to Witham and where we would as usual join the main line of the LNER.

It was a beautiful day and there was quite an assembly to see us off from Maldon. As a 15 year old (and my 16th birthday in a couple of weeks) it seemed quite an adventure and with my school friends we were full of excitement and no feelings of fear whatsoever – (I had been so homesick when evacuated initially in the previous autumn). This time I enjoyed packing my kit bag (originally bought in September 1938 or March 1939 at the time of the Munich crisis) but I was only sorry that I could not take my bicycle with me. It was quite a distance from Fambridge Road to Maldon East Railway Station and I think we had buses to convey us to the station. We had instructions to ask our billet hosts to provide food for the day, to be as nourishing as possible and wrapped as well as possible so as to keep cool in the heat (it was hot and sunny!) We were not to take any drink (no plastic containers in those days) and I suppose there was the fear of broken glass from any bottles.

Mrs Brown ingeniously provided Esme and myself with date and apple sandwiches wrapped in rhubarb leaves, and she certainly gave us a good breakfast before we set off early morning.

There would have been about 10 of us in our railway carriage, all girls – and what a journey lay ahead of us that day. It was all stops and starts once we left Witham – the day got hotter and at midday we arrived at Cambridge Railway Station – a very long stop and we were 'watered' – drinks of water provided through the carriage door from a trolley on the platform! At the time (and for the duration of the war) all signposts and indications of identification of towns and villages were all removed as there was fear of invasion by the Germans – hence no indication on railway stations as to where we were, but from time to time messages passed along the line as soon as somebody asked whenever we stopped at a station. Our journey then continued via Oxford, Pershore, Evesham and Ledbury and finally we arrived about 7.00pm at our journey's end at a small railway station at Newent in Gloucestershire – all very tired and wondering what lay ahead – as well as wondering how everybody in Maldon was coping with the new crisis. Life for us was idyllic in Gloucestershire during the next few weeks in the depths of rural England.

On looking back I realise how welcoming everybody was to me in Maldon. It was a very cold winter of 1939 to 1940 with snow and ice, but there was always plenty to do and enjoy – and I wonder now what the townsfolk really felt about us evacuees about the town (and disturbing the peace and quiet of the library etc. – the library quite intrigued me being housed in an old church!)

I enclose copies of two letters which I wrote at that time to my pen friend called Val in Australia. My pen friend at the time lived on a dairy farm near Pomona in Queensland. Our letters took six weeks each way in delivery and of course we had never met.

Our friendship blossomed because later in life her husband's job brought her to England and so we met – she had kept every letter that I wrote to her and hence after 40 years she was able to give me photocopies of what I had written to her.

Extracts from letters to Val Uhlmann, Queensland, Australia

15 November 1939

Station House, Maldon, Essex

......I was not sure whether our school would evacuate because at first we were not in a danger area; but on Sept 1st I received a notice that we were to be evacuated on 3rd September. After saying goodbye to my family I went with my brother to school on Sunday morning. We had to be there by 7.0. Of course we were all sad to have to leave home but we kept up our spirits. I haven't seen my brother since.

We were all packed into buses but nobody knew where we were going. Eventually we arrived at Chelmsford about 35 miles from London. I was billeted with a friend with some very nice people.

But a fortnight later we were moved here. There are only 350 pupils from our 700 at home and we are all billeted somewhere in the town.

The town is not very large but it has a cinema and a few shops. But it is built on a hill, and I am staying with a friend with the station master and family. The house is attached to the station and at the bottom of the hill, so we seem to be continually climbing the hill.

I am very happy here and they are all very kind to me. The station is mainly for goods and there are only a few trains. There is a grammar school here. The pupils of the school go in the morning from 9 - 12.30. We go in the afternoons from 1.30 - 4.30. But our class is still going to take school Cert in Dec so we have extra lessons in the mornings at the headmaster's house. By the time this letter reaches you I shall have finished my exams, and we get the results in January.

On Wednesday mornings we have games. I go to a Madrigal Society before hockey and we have a very nice time. We (made up of boys, girls, masters and mistresses at school) have a concert in Dec......

7 April 1940

South Woodford, London E 18

... As you will see from the above address I am at home. I have been home for the weekends quite a lot lately. You see Maldon is only just above 30 miles away from here so it only takes about 2 hours to travel home by bus or coach. I am home now for a spring holiday which lasts from April 6th - 24th.

It seems very absurd that we should be evacuated then come back to London for weekends and holidays. At school we are all doing the same. It is only when from home that you realise there is no place on this earth like home.....

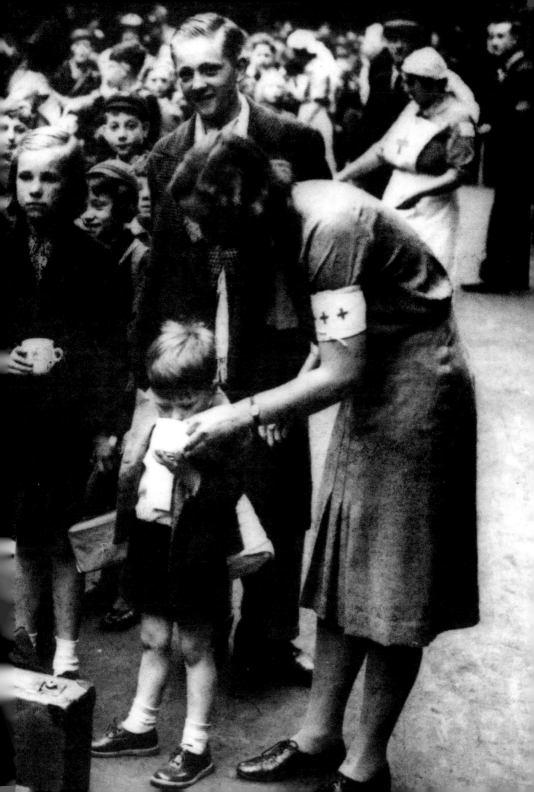

CHURCHFIELDS PRIMARY SCHOOL,
SOUTH WOODFORD, LONDON E18

Another large group came from Churchfields Primary School in South Woodford. Included in this section are the memories of three members of the same family, Arthur, Olive and Donald Cox. There is also a moving account from a lady who was evacuated with a group from Churchfields School, as an expectant mother.

"Some of my classmates were trying to look angelic so they would get picked. I thought, 'if only you knew what they are really like!'"

Interview with Mr Bernard Chamberlain, Chelmsford, Essex

Bernard was living in Chelmsford Road, South Woodford and attended Churchfields School from 1934 until the outbreak of war. On 3rd September 1939 he gathered with his school mates at Churchfields School. All his belongings were in a suitcase – he had been given a list of things to take – and he had his gas mask in a cardboard box. They were told they were being taken to a secret destination; no one knew where they were going, not even the parents.

"After we left, the parents went down to school to find out where we had gone. The caretaker wrote the one word – Maldon – on a blackboard in the playground."

They came down on red London buses. Mr Potter, their teacher, came with them. When they arrived all the pupils were all taken to a church hall.

"The children were on one side and adults on other. Some parents tried to pick out the 'nicer', angelic looking children. Some of my classmates were trying to look angelic so they would get picked. I thought, 'if only you knew what they are really like!' In fact a man called Mr Downs, a school teacher from Maldon Grammar School, was the billeting officer and he was the one who made the decisions about where we went."

For the first week he went to Victoria Road. There was a gas holder at bottom of garden with the smell of gas. Mr and Mrs Buchkan, who he stayed with, already had children of their own and had two allocated, so they were transferred to a different house.

"I was transferred to Mill Road, with a young couple, recently married – Mr and Mrs Good. He worked on the buses. The couple were very nice and made me welcome."

As he was 11 years old, he was transferred from Maldon County Primary School – where teaching was split between local children in morning and evacuees in the afternoon – to Maldon Grammar School.

Bernard has memories of playing in Promenade Park, which he says hasn't changed much since the war. He had trips to a boat yard, which he thinks was

Sadds and to Beeleigh Abbey. He was also allowed to borrow a bike and went out cycling, and remembers going to the Embassy cinema, which was in the High Street.

Bernard was a quiet, timid boy, who didn't want to be sent away from home. "I was very homesick and even though the couple I stayed with were very kind, I certainly didn't look upon the experience as a holiday, as some children seemed to."

His parents used to visit on trips organised by coach companies operating out of season. It was mainly his mother who visited, as his father and older brother were working for a solicitor's firm in Hertfordshire. His mother had stayed in Woodford with his four year old brother and 90 year old grandmother.

When he went home for Christmas in December he stayed. As this was the period of the "phoney war" many people were trickling back to London. "Some of the pupils who stayed in the district went home to Woodford and others were eventually evacuated again to Trowbridge in Wiltshire in June 1940."

Bernard spent rest of the war in Woodford, with schooling at Buckhurst Hill School. He remembers the land mine dropping in Stanley Road, South Woodford which killed a lot of people.

"On 23rd September 1943, at 9.30 at night, bombs came down on parachutes. All the lights went out, smoke and dust came down the chimney."

After the war he became a teacher, spending some time as a student teacher at Churchfields School, then going on to teach in Chingford and Walthamstow. He moved to Chelmsford when he retired.

"We were put on red London buses and set off for Maldon."

Letter from Mr Jack Davis, South Woodford, London E18

I have read in our local paper, "Wanstead and Woodford Guardian", that you would like to hear from anybody evacuated to Maldon during the war.

I was evacuated to Maldon in 1939, at the age of six. We were gathered up from Churchfields Infants School, South Woodford, and taken to the local council offices. There were quite a few of us although I can't remember any other evacuees. We were put on red London buses and set off for Maldon.

I was billeted with a family called Pitt (I understand from a recent visit that this is quite a common local name), I know where the house is but can't remember the name of the road.

I was there for about a year or so and can remember some good times in the bathing pool by the river. I have taken my family to visit Maldon quite a few times as it holds some very happy memories for me.

"I was only eight years old at the time and must still mention Wickham Bishops at least once a week."

Mr Stuart Ernest Hendry, Chelmsford, Essex – compiled from a letter and an interview

I was evacuated from Woodford to Wickham Bishops in the Maldon District. I was only eight years old at the time and must still mention Wickham Bishops at least once a week.

On September 3rd 1939, when war was declared, I went to Goldhanger with my mother and baby sister, but we only stayed a week and went home.

It was very frightening the first time when we went to Goldhanger; we were waiting at the school when the caretaker announced war had been declared and at 11.05am the siren sounded, probably the first time I had heard it. Thankfully it turned out to be a false alarm.

I came down again in October, just before my 9th birthday. We came from Churchfields School, but there were some strange children, maybe from other schools. We travelled by bus, I think it was a double decker – there may have been more than one. The locals had been expecting us a week earlier so we took them by surprise when we arrived.

I came on my own apart from a boy who was a stranger to me, his mother had asked me to look after him; his name was Stanley. I do well remember sitting in Wickham Bishops Village Hall, it seemed like we were being sorted out like cattle. One particular lady was walking up and down the aisle and I kept asking her if Stanley and I could go together. We did, with another boy Eric, (the only one in long trousers) to this lady's which was Mrs Foster-Mellior of Vine House, Carters Lane. She was wonderful to me. When we arrived at the house we sat down to a very welcome dinner. All of us wanting to press the bell for the maid as we had not seen anything like it before. Eric went home after a week and Stanley didn't stay too long. I started off on a camp bed downstairs but when the other boys went home I got a bedroom to myself.

Regarding school, we had half days at Wickham Bishops School and the village hall alternate weeks. Our teacher was Mrs Burroughs and she had an Austin Seven car. The village boys did not accept the evacuees very well, there was some name calling, and also hitting and chasing us. At the village hall we used to sing songs from the Daily Express Song Book, I still remember some of the titles. I also learnt to knit.

I cannot recall much adventure but I settled down well. I don't remember being homesick. The family I stayed with were most charming, I loved the house and yard and countryside.

I stayed roughly five months, going home for Xmas. My grandmother put a stick through my case handle to ease the weight.

I used to go with the gardener on Sunday mornings, ferreting. His name was Jim. Elsie Pearson the maid/cook had a daughter Winnie, who I have never seen since, but would love to get in touch with her again. Winnie's grandparents lived in Colchester. Winnie and myself would go out to the back before breakfast to retrieve the rabbits that had been snared; her mother used to make some wonderful rabbit pasties. There were also three fields and a small coppice which went with the house, where I used to wander regularly.

Mrs Foster-Mellior was the most charming lady. She would help sew the costumes for the Xmas play. We always went into Witham every Saturday morning by car. While at Mrs Foster-Mellior's I went to Mrs Sess-Smith's at High Hall for tea one Saturday, I had not seen so many maids in all my life. Very often on Saturday afternoons we would take the dog for a walk, probably through Colonel and Mrs Wright's orchard.

The dialect was very strong in Wickham Bishops. The children at school could not understand me when I returned. The district where I lived at home was very much open space but naturally Wickham Bishops was very much more rural but I always liked the country so did not take much notice. We did have quite a lot of snow, I suppose it would be January 1940 when Church Road was blocked to Wickham Hall.

I only remember doing one thing very wrong, the people in the cottage at the end of the garden, Mr Clay's family, had a niece evacuee staying with them. She would come and play with us during the evening, her name was Brenda. However I was taking her home one night with a torch in my hand and shone the light in the sky, and the next thing was the local policeman knocking at the door!

I also had lice in my head. Of course being very worried, I was taken to Maldon clinic by the nurse.

I cannot recall much about visits, my grandparents came once or twice as grandfather could get reduced fares as he worked for the railway. They would come to Wickham Bishops station and then walk, which was a fair way. Once I went back to London for a weekend.

I went to help out at Dick Martin's farm at Totham – Walden House Farm. I do remember going on the strawberry lorry to Tiptree and sitting in the back with Dick's grandson David who I think still lives at Walden House. You may depend some strawberries went missing.

I was not re-evacuated. I went home to Woodford when the other evacuees went to Wales. I stayed for the rest of the war at Woodford where we had shelters in the playground. If we rode bikes to school we were not allowed to ride home if there was a raid on. Much later I went with my mother and sister to Devon on for a short spell.

When I left school I decided I was going farming which lasted nearly 40 years ending up as head cowman.

I kept in touch with Mrs Foster-Mellior into the 1950's. Writing periodically and going for a weekend about twice, and she always thought of me on my birthday. When I was there she had always arranged outings, as well as going riding at Mrs Mayes at Tiptree Priory. I had a week's holiday at Wickham Bishops in 1945. She finally wrote saying that she was selling up and how she would miss her garden and house as she was going to live with her daughter because she was now getting too old. Quietly telling me I should not be hearing any more.

In a roundabout way I got in touch with Mrs Nicholls, who lived at Vine House later, this was in 1987 or 1988, and she invited my wife and I over for coffee and to see the house. I would love to know what happened to Mrs Foster-Mellior.

"Here was a tidal river, sea walls, marshes, lots and lots of mud and real fishing boats and sailing barges."

Letter from Mr Arthur Cox, Latchingdon, Chelmsford

Just before my 10th birthday, early in September 1939, I found myself with an elder brother and my younger sister, waiting at our school in South Woodford with a large crowd of other children. We were all waiting to board a London bus that was to take us to the country as evacuees. We were each carrying a gas mask in a small square cardboard box, a rolled up blanket labelled with our names and a small bag holding a few precious belongings.

I said a bus but there were in fact a whole fleet of buses and soon a long convoy of these red buses was heading out to safety far out into the country. World War II had just been declared and we were among many parties of evacuees leaving the cities. Neither we, nor our parents, had any idea where we were going or for how long we would be parted.

Apart from a time when I was four and in Waltham Cross fever hospital suffering from scarlet fever, this was the first time that I had been away from home without my parents and the evacuation must have also been a very worrying time for them. We children did at least have the excitement of a journey and possible adventure to occupy our minds.

Later that same day our buses arrived at Maldon on the Essex coast. It was not quite so very far away as we had expected. After a rather confusing assembly at what is now called Lower Plume School, my brother and I were taken to our new temporary home; a house at the eastern end of Victoria Road. I cannot recall exactly which house it was or even the name of our new foster parents – our new aunty and uncle. They were an elderly couple and suddenly to have two lively boys to care for was obviously rather upsetting for them. Our younger sister was not billeted with us but was further along Victoria Road on the same side. She was with the Keeble family.

We soon discovered that because the schools had to be shared with the Maldon children, school times were going to be half-days only – a pleasant prospect for us and one that gave us plenty of time for exploring our new surroundings. We were used to the freedom to wander and play in the country because our Woodford home was very close to Epping Forest but here, at Maldon, we found some completely new delights.

Here was a tidal river, sea walls, marshes, lots and lots of mud and real fishing boats and sailing barges. Despite strict commands to keep our shoes and boots dry, we would race down the sloping back garden and out into the Downs Road and be away. We soon discovered to our horror that our wet shoes revealed tell-tale white salt deposits and our new foster "uncle" was a martinet about clean boots – we even had to polish under the instep! I think he must have been a sergeant-major before retiring. However, his boot polishing lessons proved very useful to me later on when I was in the Army.

I recall our many attempts to catch crabs with bacon-rind on a string down at The Hythe and the scooping up of small shrimps in the boating pool further along the promenade. The very neat Promenade Park had a pond then complete with ducks but that has since been filled in. Best of all were the games on the sea-wall near the causeway to Northey Island. Here we found large heaps of old brushwood (almost haystack size if I remember correctly) where we used to dig among the rotting twigs to find old bullets. Perhaps these were old butts for rifle practice?

On some days, our teachers tried to keep us out of mischief and add to our education by taking us on organised walks. One such walk was to see the ruins of St Giles Leper Hospital in Spital Road and then via a footpath by Maldon Hall to Beeleigh Abbey. I remember that we were told off by the farmer for playing "castles" along those strange low banks of earth and straw by the farm road but how were we townies to know that those heaps contained potatoes? Once the Beeleigh area had been found, this then became our new playground. Here were the rivers and canal with lock gates and a wide weir and an overshoot for excess water. The river was still tidal up to this point where the rivers Chelmer and Blackwater almost merge together. It has changed much since then but I can still remember how it was.

My brother and I must have neglected our younger sister although I do recall occasional visits up the road to the Keeble home and once we had a trip with them down Market Hill to Fullbridge; the bridge across the Chelmer was then a temporary wooden one put up while the main bridge was being repaired – I think the war started and stopped repair work. Here we looked over a sailing barge anchored near Sadds' timber wharf and were told tales of trips with this barge loaded high with timber. I have been told recently that this barge was probably the "Dawn" owned by the Keebles. You can still see it today anchored at The Hythe.

I can remember one day when the tide was high, a sudden bustle and hustle by the river with men hurrying to pull boats up on to the banks and then a large paddle boat came up the river to tie up at The Hythe. This was one of the boats that took passengers on trips to Southend-on-Sea and Margate and it might have been the last time it ever called in at Maldon.

Although we boys enjoyed our new environment, we were not really truly happy being away from our own home. On the radio we heard the war news, which seemed mainly to be about the sinking of shipping, and we thought of our dad working at the Woolwich docks. Our mum visited us at least once I remember though it may have been more than that and we wrote home, of course, but it was not really the same as being at home with all our personal possessions.

This was the "phoney war" period, and because the German invasion hadn't happened as expected and the air raids were not of the type that were to develop later with the Blitz, by early 1940 we went back home to South Woodford. I remember the train journey home one Sunday evening; the train stopped somewhere between Maldon and Witham because there really was an air raid! We sat in the dark carriages for about an hour and tried to watch the search-lights by peeping under the window blinds. We listened to the anti-aircraft guns blasting away and wondered if the German pilots could see our train by the light coming from the steam engine funnel.

Back home, we found that there was still very little schooling for us – a few days here and there only. So we were back to our old haunts and games in the forest. Our dad was then directed to work away at the docks at places such as Swansea and Plymouth so there was little to keep the family at South Woodford. My mother eventually managed to arrange for us to move to an uncle's house at Wickford, Essex, and we were settled in there about Whitsun 1940.

To us children it was our first home move and an exciting adventure. I still have my mother's correspondence with my uncle at that time and reading these letters now reveals all her worries about us. Here, at uncle's, I met for the very first time a young cousin called Sylvia. I recall that we didn't get on too well although she and my younger sister became firm friends. Little did I know then that years later, Sylvia and I would be married to each other and living not too far from my previous evacuee home.

Maldon has never ceased to fascinate us both; for me it is because of my short evacuee period and for Sylvia because Maldon was – and still is today – famous for Sunday school outings. Although we remained at Wickford until 1983, we visited Maldon often – usually on bikes. Even when our three daughters had arrived we still came; the eldest, Nicola, on a "fairy" bike and both Sylvia and I with one each of the younger ones up behind on child seats. A long journey made even longer by taking all the side lanes to avoid the traffic.

Now we live only about five miles from Maldon and the Beeleigh area is still one of our favourite places for walks but nowadays we find ourselves introducing its delights to our grandchildren.

On visits to the town, we occasionally walk down Victoria Road or along Downs Road and I find myself looking at the houses there and puzzling over which one it was that was once my evacuee home.

"Maldon had the 'smell of the sea' and boats."

Letter from Mr Donald Cox, Wickford, Essex

We, my younger brother, Arthur, and still younger sister, Olive, were evacuated from Stanley Road at South Woodford E18. I believe we were all gathered at

Churchfields Junior School, and from there were escorted to LNER, George Lane Station, where we were boarding a train bound for Maldon. Mother was there to see us off and together with our square respirator boxes we set off to the country. I can only remember being ecstatic at going for a holiday; we were never able to afford one before then.

Eventually we arrived at what was then 'Maldon East' station where we alighted. I cannot recall by what means we were transported into town, or how and when we were put into our various groups, but I do remember arriving at an address at the east end of Victoria Road and being introduced to an elderly couple. They seemed staid in their manner and habits and I felt they did not really want the bother of children around them!

My sister Olive went to stay with some people called 'Keeble' who lived in the back end of the same road. It was where we too eventually came to after some altercation involving 'Bed Wetting' – I am not sure if it was myself or my brother who was responsible for this dreadful state of affairs! But we did become unpopular.

The 'Keebles' were a different "Kettle of Fish". Mrs Keeble I feel sure was a Yorkshire woman, with Yorkshire ideas regarding food. We never felt hungry there. Sunday dinner was traditional with roast joint with onions and vegetables. Before this we were served with thick slices of Yorkshire pudding swimming in the oil they were cooked in. I also remember sitting on the back step in the sun and shelling peas into a bowl.

I believe the "Keebles" were well known after the war for their input into yacht racing.

Our first time out in Maldon was 'discovery time' and the first find for me was tomato plants with green and orange tomatoes growing in the garden! When I smell tomato plants, even now, I'm reminded of Maldon days. The garden sloped away down hill to a gateway leading into the small road adjacent to the quay and in front of the Jolly Sailor public house.

We spent many happy hours "Beach Combing" our way to the end of the promenade. I remember some sort of rectangular pool, timber sided in which we would try to catch shrimp like creatures that swam there. Another pool we would swim in, was just below the end of the park. It was very salty and swimming in it meant being covered in white crystals. There was always a hessian covered raft in the centre to sit on.

At the end of the promenade was a small shelter with a seat inside. Sometimes we would have to sit there because of cold misty rain which blew up river. On fine days we would walk along the sea wall to an Army rifle range, a corrugated iron construction, behind which, was a mound of earth. In the earth were hundreds of spent bullets. We spent many hours digging these treasures out!

Mr Keeble owned a sailing barge which was used, so we were informed, to bring timber from Swedish ships to John Sadds' wharf near the Fullbridge. We were never fortunate enough to sail in her, but we did get shown around!

Another favourite haunt was Beeleigh Abbey, the canal, lock gates, the sort of cascade there. Turning off the main road into the lane to the abbey was so suddenly quiet and peaceful, no traffic noise.

Schooling was half daily I believe and in a council school. I cannot recall where it was situated, or much about lessons, except for gardening, and the teacher telling us at great lengths the dangers of holding a fork at knee height and taking a stab at the earth, rather than placing the fork down first then adding pressure!

Personally, my stay in Maldon was a wonderful adventure! We would go from Woodford, way into the country at weekends, long hikes to Epping, Ongar, Theydon Bois and so on, but Maldon had the 'smell of the sea' and boats. So there was no actual comparison for me.

We left Maldon because my mother was worried about the increase in bombing, mines, rockets, which fell nearby and found a place with a relative in Wickford for us all to stay till we found a place of our own. We eventually did and stayed there till the cessation of hostilities.

We never went back to Maldon till after the war and we have been there many times since. My brother-in-law lived in Granger Avenue, so we always had an excuse for a visit.

"My first memory of Maldon is watching a dog fight over the town."

Interview with Mr Stan Hawkins (Née Taylor), Wickham Bishops, Essex

Stan was evacuated from Churchfields School at seven years of age. He came down to Maldon with his uncle, who was four years older than him. He remembers travelling on the top deck of a red double decker bus, wearing a scarf and cap and carrying a gas mask. Being only seven he didn't really understand why he was there or the dangers of war.

"My first memory of Maldon is watching a dog fight over the town. I was fascinated by the planes but was pulled out of the street while I was watching because I should have been in the shelter."

He stayed with Mrs Wright in Church Street. She moved to Fitches Crescent while he was down there and Stan helped pack things up for the move. Mr Wright had a sailing barge or smack for fishing, which Stan went out on once. Mr Wright was called up into the Navy in 1942 and sadly was killed in the war.

Stan remembers Mrs Wright as a little lady with good sense of humour. Her son was younger than Stan, so they didn't play together much. The attractions of Promenade Park helped to make him feel happy and comfortable living in the district; being "a bit of a loner", he was out and about in the fields or down the "Prom" in most of his spare time.

"Where the pond is now in Promenade Park they used to have a rifle range where soldiers practised shooting. I spent a lot of time there collecting the brass bullets."

He stayed in Maldon for few months, until the school was re-evacuated to Worcester. He was billeted on a farm in Worcester for a few more months, then returned home to live in Woodford Green after his family were bombed out of their house in Stanley Road, South Woodford.

Stan now has two daughters and a son. When his children grew up he and his wife moved out, first to Heybridge, which he recalls was "just a small village" during the war, and then Wickham Bishops. Fond memories of living here as an evacuee helped influence his decision to move back to the district.

"My brothers were living in a house at the other end of the same road ... they always seemed to be cleaning their shoes."

Letter from Mrs Olive Coates (Née Cox), Goring-by-Sea, Sussex

I can remember my mother sitting up late at night sewing name tags on all our clothes and other belongings because we were due to be evacuated.

We went by bus to Maldon and when we arrived we were told to get off the bus with our gas masks on our shoulders and carrying our suitcases. We walked down the middle of the road being directed into our allotted houses, two children in each household (I think).

I remember we were woken up at night time with a strange noise; it was the air raid siren. I believe that a plane was shot down in the river the same first night.

I remember going to school in the mornings and sitting three to a desk. In the afternoons we went for walks with the teachers. We used to walk along the river banks and went to see a leper colony.

I also recall playing in the puddles in the park with the girl I lodged with – I think her name was Joyce – and attending a Roman Catholic Church on Sundays which seemed strange as I didn't understand a word of it. The service was in Latin!

My brothers were living in a house at the other end of the same road. I remember going to visit them; they always seemed to be cleaning their shoes.

I cannot remember how long we stayed at Maldon but my parents brought us home because my brother was unhappy.

We had a relative in Wickford, Essex, which was then a country market town. They offered us a home with them. So we moved from Woodford leaving my eldest brother and father behind because they were both working.

I remember the day we moved for I travelled in the removal van with the driver and his mate. We stopped at a pub called "The Fortune of War" on the Southend Road. The two men went for a drink and they bought me a huge biscuit to eat while I waited in the van for them. When we arrived at the bungalow in Wickford our cousin Sylvia came out to meet us. Seeing her for the first time I'm sure we were friends immediately and remained so ever since.

"My stay in Goldhanger was a very special time for me."

Letter from Mrs Betty F Sydes, Hastings, East Sussex

I was intrigued to read your letter in the spring issue of the "ARP 050 Reporter". I was evacuated to there for a short time.

On Sunday, 3 September 1939, all the expectant mothers, of which I was one, and mothers with children under five, had to report to the school in Churchfields, Woodford, which was where I was then living. Eventually several double-decker buses arrived and we all piled on and in due course set off – none of us at the time having the slightest idea where we were going.

We eventually arrived at Goldhanger, near Maldon. The people of Goldhanger had unfortunately been led to expect that they would be getting a group of unaccompanied schoolchildren, but despite this, they turned up trumps and billets were found for everybody.

I and another expectant mother called Madeleine were sent to the pork butcher, Mr Scobell, who had a house in High Street, Goldhanger. Mr Scobell didn't have a shop, but adjacent to his house he did have a small, newly constructed building, which was where he cut up the pig carcasses ready for him to deliver in his van.

He was a German who had been made a prisoner of war in England during the First World War, had married an English girl who at the time had been in service, and he had remained in England ever since. His wife was a most delightful looking person. She had a wonderfully fresh complexion, just like apple blossom.

It really was a lovely billet. Not surprisingly, as far as meat was concerned, we only ate various cuts of pork, but I didn't ever find it too rich, and there were always plenty of home grown vegetables to go with it. Mr Scobell had what he called his field garden – an allotment at the top of the street, which was where he grew vegetables.

Mr and Mrs Scobell had two sons, one of 21 who was in the Army and Alfred who was 14. Every day at tea-time, Alfred sat down and ate a whole ridge cucumber from the field garden.

All the water for drinking had to be fetched from the pump at the top of the street, and I have a lovely snapshot of Mr Scobell and Alfred standing by the pump, with the container on wheels. The water used for washing ourselves was so soft, that it was very difficult to wash the soap off.

One occasion which happened during my stay in Goldhanger, and which particularly stands out in my mind, was when all we evacuees were invited to tea by the novelist Marjorie Allingham. She lived in Tolleshunt D'Arcy, in a lovely old house, which I remember as having a very big kitchen with an Aga cooker in it. Marjorie Allingham herself looked rather like a figure from a fairy tale. She was wearing a long black dress and she had a little white apron over it. It was a very pleasant afternoon.

A problem which arose, was where would expectant mothers go during confinement and subsequent to confinement? The powers that were, solved the problem by taking over an empty house on the road between Goldhanger and Tollesbury. They also managed to find enough furniture for me, Madeleine and some other mothers with little children, to be able to occupy the house. The idea was that these other mothers would do the cooking for, and look after, us mothers with our new babies. In addition, a retired nurse was found, and she came in to see us each day. Consequently, we had regular, expert attention.

On the 3rd of October 1939, exactly one month after we had arrived in Goldhanger, my son was born at 1.30pm.

Madeleine and I had been out walking by the side of Goldhanger Creek, when I suddenly had the feeling that I had to get back. Madeleine got the local midwife and I was whisked off to the house on the road to Tollesbury. The midwife had some difficulties with the bed which was there, because it was so sunken in the middle it was more like a hammock. However she got a board which had been covering the bath, and she put it under the mattress and it solved the problem.

After the birth, Mrs Scobell from the billet came in Mr Scobell's delivery van to visit me, and she had brought me a little stone coloured vase with some honeysuckle in it. I treasured that vase for years, but sadly must have mislaid it at sometime.

My stay in Goldhanger was a very special time for me. It had been a delightful month. The weather had been perfect. Madeleine and I had been out picking blackberries, and in spite of the war, my entrance into the realms of motherhood had been very happy and my son was beautiful.

THE ESSEX CHRONICLE SEPTEMBER 1939·

MFORD SESSION

, Esq. (in the chair), Mrs
nd Sir Edward Wilshaw

IBILITY FOR HORSES

Martin, Lodge Avenue,
immoned for ill-treating a
 it in an unfit condition
Crown Street, Dagenham,
iminal was summoned for
nce

iewood, of the R.S.P.C.A.,
ist 12 he was cycling near
ublic-house at Rainham
tin driving a pony mare
ll covered cart. Witness
mplaint that this pony has
 a sore " Martin pulled
showed him an old callous
iof sore. Witness examined
was aged, but in good
Under the saddle he found
was wet, and adhering to
felt The sore was painful
know how it is at holiday
s bad as that when I left
his morning It must have
less later saw Arthy, who
I am responsible" When
reported he said, "It is
nd a horse out like that I
 out. My men have said
ut it"
nts' behalf it was stated
 seen the animal for three
re the responsibility of his
in had been treating the
ne, and it was now quite
ed
£1, with costs 4/- each.

OF JUDGMENT.

 Charter Street, Gilling-
immoned for driving a car
rous to the public and/or
nd attention, also for not
en constructed of safety

at the defendant took a
ffords Road, Romford, on
me with a car driven by
Hamilton Avenue, Colier

was the first time he had
road, which was not well
aching car had only its
ng little illumination. The
 ie could give was that it
idgment. Dealing with the
he was under the impres-
of the windscreen was of

 t dangerous driving was
careless driving the defen-
with costs £1/1/-. On the
was fined 10/-

G TRAFFIC ISLAND.

 approached the traffic
orner at too fast a speed
nd to have skidded, Sidney
own Road, Romford, was
eless driving.
 e did not apply his brakes
when he realised he was
the island too quickly he
the machine skidded.

EXPECTANT MOTHERS
VAST VOLUME OF WORK
GIFTS NEEDED.

The vast amount of work that is being
carried out in regard to evacuated expectant
mothers was described to THE ESSEX
CHRONICLE by the County Medical Officer of
Health, Dr. W. A. Bullough, on Tuesday.
He said:—

" During August, arrangements were made
with the Government and the London
County Council to evacuate about 260 expectant mothers into Essex. Arrangements were accordingly made to put
the women into suitable billets in reception areas, and in improvised maternity
homes. On the outbreak of war, however, a
much greater evacuation of expectant
mothers into Essex took place; at the
moment we know of more than 1,000, and
names are still pouring in. Accordingly, the
scheme had to be expanded and revised, and
so far we have coped with the situation without a single mishap. Offers of country
mansions have been made very liberally, and
particular mention should be made of Lord
Edward Hay, of Hill Hall; Theydon Mount;
Mrs. J. T. Wigan, Danbury Park; the Hon.
Rupert Blyth, Campions, Harlow; and Sir
Wm. Courtauld.
" At the present moment there are improvised maternity homes at Hill Hall (50
beds), Moulsham Grange (25 beds), Danbury
Park (20 beds), Lawford Place (35 beds),
Michaelstowe Convalescent Home (50 beds),
Campions (10 beds), the William Julien
Courtauld Hospital, Braintree (10). The
East End Maternity Hospital has practically
transferred itself to Hill Hall. Writtle Park
is being hastily furnished and equipped, and
it is hoped to have it open in a fortnight's
time.
" In some cases generous offers of country
mansions as hostels have been accepted
gladly. Among these are : Wilderness House,
Ongar (Mrs. Denis Buxton); White House,
Ongar (Mr. and Mrs. Lees); D'Arcy House,
Tolleshunt D'Arcy (Mrs. Youngman Carter);
Birch Hall, Theydon Bois (Mrs. Gerald
Buxton).
" These hostels will be of great assistance in
providing suitable homes while the mothers
are waiting, and after they have had their
babies in the improvised maternity homes
There must be many expectant mothers who
have not yet notified their presence in the
county, and they may not know what to do.
Each woman should speak either to the
district nurse, the health visitor, the billeting
officer, the clerk to the local authority, or,
in a last resort, write to me at the County
Hall, Chelmsford. Billeting officers to the
local authorities have been exceedingly busy
and industrious in finding suitable homes for
the expectant mothers. Mr. R. W. Revans, the
Assistant Director of Education, has super-
vised and co-ordinated the work of the
billeting officers, and has most successfully
undertaken a very difficult task. Gifts of
fruit, vegetables, babies' clothing, etc., will
be gladly received at the improvised maternity homes mentioned, or at the County
Hall. I need hardly mention how valuable
this particular work is."

Bates, Sliman, Mayes ; Phillips, Wright,
Palethorpe, Ramage, Burley.

It is expected that "Bill" Edrich, the
England and Middlesex cricketer and former
Tottenham Hotspur footballer, who has been
signed on by Chelmsford City, will report
for duty at Chelmsford after the Scarborough
cricket festival, which terminates on Sept. 12.

CHELMSFORD CITY'S TEAMS

For their games to-morrow Chelmsford City
have selected the following teams:—
v. CHELTENHAM CITY—Southern League. At
Cheltenham, 3.30: Dolman; Turton, Wood;

BRENTWOOD PETTY SESSION

YESTERDAY.

Before H. F. Chamen (chairman), A. J.
Baker, and T. F. Rawle, Esqrs.

TWO LEARNERS—George Hearn, commer-
cial traveller, The Drive Walthamstow, was
summoned for driving a motor car without
due care at South Weald on July 26—Supt
Whiting said Mr G Pitter, a learner driver,
was undergoing a test He was turning
slowly out of Milton Road into Victoria Rd,
when a car, driven by defendant, travelled
across the road to its off side and collided
with the front part of Mr Pitter's car. Defendant told P.c Wright that the car came
out without warning, and he was unable to
avoid a collision — Evidence was given by
George C. Pitter, Tavistock Gardens, Ilford,
John Simmons, driving examiner, Junction
Road Brentwood; and P.c Wright—Defendant said he pulled out to pass a lady and
child walking in the road and at that
moment the other car came out of the side
road without warning, and drove across his
path Witness was also a learner driver—
Stanley C. Bailey, Highams Park, the com-
petent driver who was accompanying defendant, also gave evidence — The Chairman
said there was conflict of evidence, and the
case would be dismissed

THOBY LANE COLLISION—Basil L. Briggs,
van driver, Holly Tree Cottages, Chappel,
was charged with driving without due care
at Mountnessing on July 16—Supt. Whiting
said Albert L. Cormack, of Dagenham, w.
cycling towards Chelmsford, and was passing
the opening to Thoby Lane when a car
driven by defendant turned across the main
road and collided with the cycle. The cycle
was damaged, but Cormack was not hurt
Defendant told the cyclist that his view was
blocked by a car, and he did not see him—
Fined £3 and £1/12/6 costs.

Before J. T. West (chairman), and D. Cor-
nish, Esqrs.

CYCLE AND SUIT—Victor A. J. Lewis, 39,
of no fixed abode, was charged with stealing a gentleman's suit at Warley on August
23 also stealing a bicycle white billee at
Warley on April 28 — David McKuigen,
Albert Street, Warley, said defendant lived
at the same lodgings as himself for some
time—On August 23rd witness missed a suit
which had been hanging on the door of his
bedroom — Det c on. Sheppard said Lewis
admitted taking the suit—Albert A Weaver
Glenwood Cafe, Arterial Road, Little Wat-
ley, said he employed defendant last April
Lewis borrowed his bicycle one day, and
witness did not see him or the bicycle again
—Defendant handed a written statement to
the Bench, and said he had nothing to add—
Defendant, who was stated to have had previous convictions, was sentenced to three
months' imprisonment on each charge, the
terms to run consecutively.

VARIOUS—Stanley E. May, Hazeline Rd,
Goodmayes, for exceeding the speed limit at
South Weald, was fined 30/-.——John E
Lavender, Great Eastern Street, Brentwood,
for causing ballast to be conveyed on an un-
verified vehicle, was fined £1 — Pte Regi-
nald L Vickery, 3rd Battalion, Royal Tank
Regt. Warminster for driving a motor vehicle without a licence was fined 10/-; and for
aiding and abetting the offence, Henry Cow

ST

Before
Mrs.
E. F.

A
The P
Charles
nesbury
car in a
on July
Lynne
defenda
of a car
second
Brigade
entirely
looking
at the c
Mr I
car will
his view
other c
The c
missed
costs or
was not
that he
would v

After
ing his
permitte
worth w
dall, of
was gra
his car
A fine
on Herb
ley, to

DR
Miss
Green I
7/6 cost
without
Greathe
permitti

A fin
Sayer, o
for driv
Sawbrid

IN

SAD

Mr.
Laura
on West
that th
Robert
plane w
to drive
night
R.A.F
Mr.
employe

CHEL
Ingatest
Nora E
G Rev

OTHER WOODFORD SCHOOLS

Children were evacuated to Maldon District from many of the schools in the Woodford area, several are mentioned here by name, such as Cowslip Road, Ray Lodge and St Anthony's Roman Catholic School. Other people can't remember the name of their school after all these years but know they were living in the area.

Two of the evacuees in this chapter, Joyce and John Bowyer, actually met up in later life to discover that they had not only lived and attended schools in the same district; they had both been evacuated to Heybridge during the war. It seems that fate kept pushing them together until romance finally blossomed. They are now married and living close to Maldon.

"We came down on a London bus, and my main concern was that my sister would not be travel sick."

Interview with Joyce Bowyer (Née Peacock), Cock Clarks, Essex

"I was evacuated with my sister Molly who was six years old, from Woodford Green. I was 12 years old but I came down with my sister's school, Ray Lodge, rather than my own school, St Barnabas, so I could look after her. We came down on a London bus, and my main concern was that my sister would not be travel sick."

Joyce remembers going to a hall when they arrived, to be allocated a billet. She and Molly went to Waterview by the side of the canal, near The Benbridge Hotel at Heybridge.

"We stayed with Mr and Mrs Cutts. They had no children and had relatives who owned a little bakehouse in Holloway Road. I remember on our first day there was an air raid. They were very nice people, they had an extended family and they all made a fuss of us. I liked being on the canal, watching the barges that came through being pulled by horses."

They only had a very short stay at Heybridge, about a fortnight, during which time they wrote several letters home. Joyce's letters reveal remarkable maturity for such a young girl whilst Molly's letter gets straight to the point. For a brief time Joyce went to school in the afternoon at Heybridge, sharing the school with the local children who went in the morning. Shortly after starting back at school Joyce's mother made arrangements for the children to leave Heybridge and go down to Buckinghamshire to stay with her sister.

While they were gone their house in Woodford was requisitioned for a homeless family who had a distinct taste in decor. "All the house, including the lino, was painted green. Even the fireplace was painted green. Luckily the next family which stayed in the house stripped it all off. We eventually got the house back in 1947."

Joyce and Molly with Mrs Cutts
at Heybridge

Copies of letters written by Joyce and Molly to their mother

4 Sept 39 – Waterview, Heybridge

Dear Mum,

We are having a lovely time here. Every evening we are going to have a gas mask drill and Molly doesn't mind having hers on.

Uncle Bill as we call him is a baker, and there is a bakehouse in his garden. We have seen him making the bread and Molly's weeny loaf has just come out of the oven. Molly has been to our house selling bread just now. She's got a basket, an apron and a book and pencil. She is enjoying herself. She has been using my pyjama top because it has been so hot. So when you come, please bring her a nightdress.

There are two dogs here. One is a terrier (Rover) and what a terror he is. The other is Thax, a big golden retriever and if he runs at you he can knock you over. Both of them are very nice and love to have a game with you.

We are going to the school tomorrow to have a medical inspection. There is a French walnut tree here and the nuts will be falling sometime next month. The nuts are much larger than an English walnut.

The sirens woke us up last night and we came downstairs. Mr Cutts gave us some orange wine which we did not like and when the all-clear sounded we went back to bed. I did not go to sleep till about a quarter of an hour afterwards, but Molly seemed to go off all right. Aunt Daisy and Mrs Cutts did not go to sleep again. Molly and I sleep in a double bed. I have got a sore neck and so did Molly have, but Mrs Cutts put on some embrocation and hers went.

Yesterday afternoon we went for a five mile walk with uncle Bill. We brought home some sloes for Mrs Cutts to make wine with. There was such a lot to see that we didn't feel tired until we got home. Uncle Bill is going to take us out on the river one day.

Love from, Molly and Joyce

(PS) Hurry up and come down.   **Molly**

Waterview, Heybridge

Dear Mum,

We are getting on nicely with our gas mask drill and I have a medium size one now. We do not know when we are starting school yet, but Columbine says they are starting in a fortnight. Columbine is at Heybridge Basin, about a mile away and is the seaside. I do not know about the fishing but I suppose there are fishes in the river because I have seen many people fishing. I have seen some girls I know round here and one day we are going to see Frances and John. The blackberries are ripe and we have been eating handfuls of them.

We might be going to the seaside at Maldon for a picnic to day. Miss Ray and Mrs Double are next door to us with Geoffrey and Michael Hawkes. I have 21/2d in pocket money left and Molly has 7d. We've had 2d given to us. We are sending a photograph of Thax to you.

Love, Molly and Joyce

12 September 1939 – Waterside, Heybridge

Dear Mum,

We are starting school on Wednesday (tomorrow) afternoon at 1 o'clock, coming out a quarter past 4. I am in Miss Reeves class. We go in the afternoon while the Heybridge children go in the morning. We enjoyed our picnic very much and we both went paddling in the lake. Molly has only spent 1d on ice cream and she had 2d given to which left 7d.

Thanks for money which I needed very much. We are about 10 mins walk from Maldon East and Heybridge station. It is twenty to nine now and I will finish to-morrow. We feed the chickens daily and take the eggs from them. Yesterday there were two eggs and we have just eaten them for breakfast. No eggs yet as it is too early but we have collected some feathers. There is one black one and the other nine are brown. Uncle Albert has 32 chickens but they are young and do not lay eggs yet.

We have both got a cold and our noses keep running so we have to run after them. What number do Frances and John live in London Road, please and then we can go to see them.

Love from, Molly and Joyce

X X X X X X X X X X X

Dear Mum,
    I went paddling
the other day and I want to
come home. We are starting
school to-morrow and I am
in Mrs Doubles class.
    Love from
    Molly
X X X X X X. ps. I have sent a feather
        & my name's on it.

"Aunt" Daisy and Thax in their garden at Heybridge

"There was an outhouse and garden on the opposite side of the road to the house, with the toilet in a bucket. This was a bit of a culture shock as I came from a modern house with a 'proper' bathroom."

Interview with Mr (Frederick) John Bowyer, Cock Clarks, Essex

John, who was known as Fred at school, lived at Woodford Green, Essex. He was 12 years old and attending St Barnabas School. He was evacuated with his younger sister, Kathleen, from Woodford Bridge Junior School.

John remembers being in Woolworth's in Walthamstow buying a giro-top and running for the shelter when he first heard a siren, so he thinks he came down later than the start of the war.

"One of my earliest memories of arriving in Heybridge, was hearing sirens going and seeing a plane fly over that looked like it was flying straight up Goldhanger Road."

"I think we went to the school hall when we arrived, then I was taken to a house, Barnfield Cottages, behind a garage in Heybridge. I was separated from Kathleen and billeted with a younger boy. We stayed with Mr and Mrs Shortland. They had children who were older than me. Their eldest son Ivor was in the Army. Peter was in the Air Force and was killed during the war and is buried in the local cemetery. The other brothers, Bruce and Bernard, were still at home and Mr Shortland worked at Bentalls."

"There was an outhouse and garden on the opposite side of the road to the house, with the toilet in a bucket. This was a bit of a culture shock as I came from a modern house with a 'proper' bathroom."

John, who had only seen milk delivered in bottles, also remembers the novelty of the milkman, who came round with milk churns and put the milk into a jug. He also remembers Horlicks tablets which you could buy for five a penny.

His sister stayed nearby, also in Barnfield Cottages, then moved to Colchester Road with Mr and Mrs Clark. They were so taken with Kathleen that they wanted to keep her and asked her parents if they could adopt her (they said no).

At first he went to school in Heybridge. They put on a play at Heybridge School and he was Robin Hood. He enjoyed playing the part and was particularly proud of his rosewood bow. He then moved to Maldon Grammar School. The journey was a bit of a trek.

"The bus used to frequently break down on Market Hill and we had to walk to school up the steep hill. There was a bit of bullying going on by local boys. We were treated as Cockneys and Londoners, but in fact weren't; coming from a fairly rural area."

After school he went rowing on the canal and played on the field at the back of the cottages. He recalls visiting Heybridge Basin and the salt works and the wrecks on the estuary. He also went down to the fruit farm down Goldhanger Road.

"The farmer gave out apples, but you had to eat the lot, including the pips!"

Another memory is of the barrage balloon which came along one day and shorted out all the lights by pulling down the electricity cable.

His parents visited from time to time, but mostly his father came alone. "On one occasion my father came to visit and went back in thick 'pea souper' fog. He followed the road home by hanging on to the fences."

John and his sister went back after a couple of months, in time for his 13th birthday in November. His sister wanted to stay at home so he went back to school in Woodford then got a job as errand boy and later went into the grocery trade. Like many of the other evacuees, the transition from being a child who was sent away for protection to being an adult, fit to go to war, was very fast.

"At 17 I had a medical for the Army but wasn't called up because I was doing 'essential work', working on the railway. I was standing on Stratford Station when I saw the first buzz bomb. We all thought we had shot down a German plane, and cheered."

He met Joyce at a mutual friend's 21st birthday party. Despite going to the same schools and being evacuated to same area, they hadn't met. Romance blossomed, and they married and eventually came back to Essex to live. One of their sons now lives at Heybridge Basin, the other at South Woodham Ferrers.

"We only stayed for nine months as by then the German planes were offloading their bombs on the east coast and it was decided to be unsafe and we had to be re-evacuated."

Letter from Mrs Joan Philp (Née Lodge), Lower Tregunnon, Launceston

I have seen your letter in the "Essex Countryside Magazine", I was one of those evacuees, billeted in Tenterfield Road, we only stayed for nine months as by then the German planes were offloading their bombs on the east coast and it was decided to be unsafe and we had to be re-evacuated.

I thoroughly enjoyed my stay in Maldon, I was 11 at the time and came from Woodford on the outskirts of London. We came from Cowslip Road Junior School in South Woodford. We arrived the day war broke out in a double decker bus along with our emergency rations:- two packets of biscuits, a tin of milk and a tin of corned beef. We each had a label tied to our lapels identifying us and if my memory serves me right, our gas masks in cardboard boxes hung round our necks with string.

I went to the senior school in Wantz Road, where the father of the gym mistress, Miss Binder, grazed sheep in the adjoining field. We had quite a lot of snow that winter but we still had to play netball amidst high drifts.

I often went to the "Prom"; and enjoyed the paddling pool and boating lake, also walking along the River Blackwater, watching the fishermen and boats and where you could buy fresh dabs threaded on a wire.

I used to do the weekly shopping at the Co-op at the top of Market Hill and on Saturdays we always had hot meat pies for dinner from Janet's Pantry just around the corner from Tenterfield Road. There was a drill hall in this road, which I believe was a cul-de-sac, there was also a short cut through to the High Street.

The man I was billeted with worked at Crittall's glass factory in Heybridge but unfortunately he died during the war.

I also remember going to Beeleigh quite often, and watching the eels in the locks. I attended Harvest Festival at the Salvation Army Hall, that was great fun to me.

I visited Maldon several times after the war, took my own children there and corresponded with my foster mother until her death, just a few years ago. It was all rather a long time ago, but I still have many happy memories.

"I have mixed memories of my time in Maldon."

Letter from Mrs Dorothy Bolder, Cleethorps, South Humberside

I was 10 years old in the October after I was evacuated to Maldon in the summer of 1939. At that time I lived in Woodford Green and I attended St Anthony's RC School in Woodford Wells. I was evacuated with a group from my school. I travelled down to Maldon with the group but I was on my own, not with my mother. (I was the only one of my family to be evacuated as my two brothers were a lot older than me and they both fought in the war). We travelled to Maldon by bus.

When we arrived in Maldon, I can remember that we were taken to a school for selection. When our names were called, we went with whichever family wanted us. I can remember that there was only myself and one boy left, and we went with a Mrs XX *(name withheld – editor)*.

Mrs XX was a newly-wed and did not really want to take in any evacuees, only she had to as the family who lived in the house before her had volunteered to take in evacuees and their name had not been struck off the register when they moved. The impression which I had formed was that Mrs XX thought that she should have been treated like a "LADY" as she was a married woman.

I went to the school in Maldon for a week before the nuns who had accompanied us children decided to hold private classes for us. We were then taught privately by the nuns. I was only in Maldon for three months before my mother took me back home with her. I was not re-evacuated anywhere else and I spent the rest of the war around the Woodford area.

After the war I didn't keep in touch with the people I was evacuated with or the people to whom I was evacuated. I did however go back once in 1962, when I took my own family there for a day to see a lady who I liked very much, a Mrs Markham. She made us all very welcome. We then went to see Mrs XX, but she was not very interested and she kept us talking on the doorstep, not inviting us in.

I must admit that I have mixed memories of my time in Maldon. I didn't understand at the time why we were being evacuated and I was frightened to begin with. Having said this, I wasn't homesick. My mother came down to visit me a few times, on Sundays. As a place, I really liked Maldon. The only blot was Mrs XX. She didn't like me in particular, and I didn't like her. Her husband, what I can remember of him, was nice. We didn't see a lot of him as he was working during the day.

Maldon was not too different really from what I was used to. People think that coming from London, everything would be built up and very busy. We actually lived on the outskirts of London and although it was busy, it was a different type. The pace was not so hectic. Maldon was also busy but not hectic. Although it is a sea-side place, the two districts have a lot in common, although when I was there, it was out of season and on the quiet side.

I have a few very happy memories and some not so happy. I can remember that the lady who lived next door to us, (I cannot remember her name) was very kind to me and the other boy who was evacuated with me. I especially remember the day that war was declared. Her son was an officer in the RAF, and on this day, he took me and the little boy evacuee out for the day with his mother and other friends in his open seated MG Tourer. We were very excited. I can remember going to Clacton and then to an apple factory. All of which was new and exciting for us. However, when we arrived home, Mrs XX forbade us to have anything to do with this kindly family. She gave the reason as we were being a nuisance by being in the way.

The other family which I liked very much were Mrs Flo Markham and her brothers. Mrs Markham was a rock-maker and she sold the rock from a little shop. Her brothers helped her make the rock. I remember that one of her brothers kept ferrets. He let us look at his ferrets and hold them. He also took the time and trouble to show us how to make the rock. Once again having made friends with a kindly family, we were forbidden to have anything to do with them as once again we were getting in the way.

The most overriding memory I have of my time spent at Mrs XX's is being accused of bed-wetting. I shared a bed with another girl, but she came from a "better" family than my own. This girl would wet the bed, but Mrs XX would not believe that anyone from her background could so such a thing, and therefore I was always blamed for it.

I remember that the last time my mother came to visit, she brought a new dressing gown for me. However, when it was time for her to go, I went with her. She said that I didn't have to stay any longer. I think that if I had gone to a different type of family, perhaps one which was slightly older, my time would have been more enjoyable.

I returned home to Woodford with my mother and spent some time there before moving to Grimsby after my father died. I married a Grimsby man, had four children and have spent my life here ever since.

"The cucumbers stand out in my memory; we had never seen knobbly ones before."

Mrs Cynthia Saggers (Née Stevenson), Woodford Green, Essex - compiled from a letter and an interview

I lived in Woodford Green and still do. I and my brother, Albert, were evacuated to Goldhanger. We came from Woodford Green Primary School. I was just five or six and my brother was nine.

We stayed with two spinster sisters. My brother thinks we stayed at a vicarage because he remembers a vicar and lots of prayers, but I don't have any recollection of that. I do recall they lived in a cottage with a driveway up to it and used to grow knobbly cucumbers round their front door. The cucumbers stand out in my memory; we had never seen knobbly ones before and we were a bit apprehensive about eating them in case they were poisonous.

Although nothing seemed to happen around there they made us put our gas masks on every time there was an air raid warning and we couldn't take them off until we heard the all-clear. We did not settle down very well and were very homesick so my mother brought us back. There was certainly more action here, we stayed through the Blitz, but we all survived.

I later married a Woodford boy, had a son and ended up living just a few streets away from where I was born.

"The granddad kept ferrets for rabbiting and we were terrified of the white wiggley things."

Letter from Mrs Mary Crockett (Née Barrett), Woodford Green, Essex

I have just seen your notice in the "Woodford Guardian". The old saying "I was there" as an evacuee.

We left Ray Lodge Infant/Junior School in Snakes Lane, Woodford the weekend war was declared and our headmistress Mrs Popperwell was at the gates as the coaches pulled up; us with our masks, labels, small case and sandwich and fruit. No one seemed to know where we were going. As young children – I was nine years old, my next door neighbours Eileen and Bobby Snell were a little older – we wanted to stay together.

We arrived in Heybridge. It might as well have been the moon for all we knew, it wasn't home. I remember going in a church hall and we were allocated to various homes. Eileen and myself went to a Mrs Tucker in the main road and Bobby and another boy a few doors away in a house with a laundry at the back.

We had to leave after a very short time when the daughter of the house became very ill. We were as happy as could be expected except for one thing, the granddad kept ferrets for rabbiting and we were terrified of the white wiggley things.

We moved a few doors away to a Miss Clarey, an elderly lady with housekeeper companion who was only known as Prissy. Miss Clarey was something to do with, I believe, a flour mill that stands high up on the hill, Maldon way. And although she was very kind she had no ideas on young children.

We used to walk down a lane and along the canal banks. School to start with was morning one week, afternoon the next, some lessons in the church hall, others in our party were brothers (I think twins), the Dellar boys.

Although we weren't town children we all hated the bats (you don't see them around here). We walked around with things on our head, scarves, hats, anything (so they didn't catch in our hair). Probably local children had told us to.

Very many of us came home for Xmas '39, as nothing was happening. Eileen, Bobby and I never went back. We kept in touch for quite a while but then the Blitz and with everything else we lost touch eventually, with our "temporary mothers".

It certainly was an experience for a young girl. I'll never forget.

"It was there that we learnt that crab apples are not for eating!"

Letter from Mr Ken Sanders, Cromer, Norfolk

Having read your request for ex-evacuees to Maldon in the "ARP 050 Reporter" News and Views page I thought that you may like to know of my brother Norman's and my experience over about 10 to 11 weeks stay in Maldon as evacuees.

At the outbreak of war we lived in South Woodford, attending Cowslip Road School and our parents were given the chance for us to leave the area for safety. After much debate they agreed it would be for our best.

On the appointed day we assembled at the school with our gas masks and suitcase and a bag of food, wearing our best clothes. To us it was like going on a day outing except we had a case in which was writing paper and home addressed stamped envelopes.

Arriving in Maldon we debussed and were made to form a line by our teachers, then people came along and looked at our labels which had our names and home address plus our age on them. They then started to pick us out and handed us to those who would be having us stay with them. We were to stay with Mr and Mrs Turner at Market Hill. They were an elderly couple with a daughter who we believe was a nurse and Mr Turner was/had been the town Mayor (if our memory is correct). I remember their name and address because I wrote it in my bible at the time and still have the bible. They looked after us well until one day we were told that we had to leave as their daughter was being posted and they were too old to look after two young boys.

We were then sent to another house and the people again looked after us until something happened in the family which meant we were on the move again. This time on arriving at the house our teacher decided it was not suitable so off we went again.

The house we were billeted at this time was on a river bank and to reach it we had to cross a rickety bridge made of loose boards. When we wrote to our parents and told them about this they could not sleep at night expecting to hear that we had drowned. A short time later they came down and took us home for their peace of mind.

All the time we had missed our parents but had enjoyed playing football especially when we played on the bowling green, scrumping in the apple orchards, playing on the old sunken barges, being invited to play at the school playground. It was there that we learnt that crab apples are not for eating!

The memory which has been with me from those days was going early in the morning to the bakers to bring back hot rolls for breakfast, as they say in Norfolk, they were "bootiful".

Looking back now we were well looked after and in a way enjoyed our stay and thank the people of Maldon for putting themselves out so much to look after other people's kids.

"A fire bomb fell opposite to where we stayed."

Compiled from letters from Mrs Pat Southgate (Née Hussey), Frinton-on-Sea, Essex

I was evacuated to Maldon with my two sisters, Eileen and Sheila, and my brother, Joseph. It was at the beginning of the war. We lived at South Woodford, E18.

We came with St Anthony's RC School, Mornington Road, Woodford Green, with the nuns and travelled by coach. When we arrived I remember we were taken to London Road and our names called out. My oldest sister and I went with Mr and Mrs Daisy and Frank Smith from London Road. Mr Smith was a builder. In fact he built the lovely house himself.

My younger sister and brother were with Mr and Mrs William and Beatie Cranmer, who lived in the big house opposite the police station, he was a policeman. They were lovely people. I remember they had a rocking horse which we used to play on in what was like a stable in the garden. They said we could have it but when we went home we had no means of transport for such a big thing. How my little grandchildren would love it now, I wonder what became of it. The thing I remember most is the first night the siren sounded and a fire bomb fell opposite to where we stayed in London Road. It was very frightening.

Mr and Mrs Keebles (related to the Smiths) had a farm and we spent many happy times there. They also had a shop in Spital Road which we liked to visit. I remember the black lolly pops Beryl's mum gave us.

We went to Maldon County Primary. The nuns stayed next door to us in London Road. I can't remember how long we stayed, it was for quite a time. When it got a bit quieter we went home but were evacuated again to Yorkshire when the flying bombs started.

My mother used to come to visit us when she could afford it to Maldon. There were always tears when it was time to say goodbye.

We used to love going down the "Prom" and going swimming. We did keep in contact for a time when we went home but then stopped writing. In 1965 we moved from Woodford, my husband and I went to live in Tolleshunt D'Arcy with my two children, Mandy and Sandra, and lived there for four years and from there to Suffolk Road, Maldon and stayed for 18 years by which time we had three children.

I did get in contact with Mr and Mrs Smith also Mr and Mrs Cranmer who then lived in Acacia Drive. Mrs Cranmer was very happy to meet my family. Sadly they have all passed away now.

We have lived in Frinton for eight years and love it. My eldest daughter is always visiting many friends in Maldon who we all keep in touch with.

"I can remember a dog being stuck in the ice on the pond in the park."
Compiled from letters from Mr Stanley Clarke, Walthamstow, London E17

I was evacuated to Maldon September 1939. I was there for a few months. I was seven years old. My younger brother and I stayed at a house named Rosemary Cottage, it was near some allotments.

I can remember going down to the River Blackwater; we walked along the sea wall, at low tide you could walk across to one of the islands. I can remember a dog being stuck in the ice on the pond in the park, the side of the River Blackwater. The owner of the dog was able to get him out, after a while the dog was OK.

I can remember the boat-building sheds along the edge of the River Blackwater. We would be with a group of school children. As far as I can think back, I never went to school in Maldon.

We only stayed in Maldon a few months, we were moved from there to Worcestershire on a farm. We stayed on the farm until the war ended. I went to the village school.

After the war I came back to Woodford Green where I went to school in Highams Park E4. I left school at the age of 14, after that we moved to Walthamstow E17, when I started work, I have lived in Walthamstow ever since.

"To us it was like going on a day outing. . ." Ken Sanders

Photograph – Imperial War Museum

THE PRIVATE EVACUEES

⸎

Many families made their own arrangements to send their children to places of relative safety during the war rather than take part in the mass evacuation arranged through the schools. Of the people who contacted me a fairly large group came as "private" evacuees to stay with family or friends in the district. These were the people who stayed the longest, remaining after all the others were re-evacuated elsewhere. One or two never went home and still live in the district today.

"I still get a yearning to come back there so I must have been happy."

Letter from Mr George Goldsmith, Exeter, Devon

I noticed your appeal in the "News of The World". I think I was the first evacuee. My aunt, a Miss Mary Brown was in Maldon for a holiday taking me with her, she had a friend who lived there and often used to take me. I think the war had just started the last time she took me and it was arranged that I stay with my aunt's friend and her husband. I believe I was nine years old and the names of the people I stayed with were Eddie and Alice Gooch and they lived at Volwick Avenue.

While I was there they had three more boys billeted there. I don't know how long I stayed but they went back to their homes quite a while before I did.

My address at the time was Bethnal Green in the East End of London. We lived over a bag wash shop, which my mother used to look after.

I can remember the day I left Maldon I was helping Eddie on his new allotment at the bottom of the road when my mum and dad came down for me. It was before the war ended because doodlebugs were still coming over. When I got back to London my parents had been bombed out in Bethnal Green and we moved to Hanwell in Middlesex.

I have been back to Maldon twice for the day and met Alice Gooch's sister and her husband and son Peter Vince, who I used to play with. Alice and Eddie had died and the sister lived two doors away in Volwick Avenue.

I still get a yearning to come back there so I must have been happy whilst there.

"All the pots and pans were pinging as the bullets hit them."

Interview with Mrs Patricia Barnes (Née Sexton), Harlow, Essex

Patricia was just five years old when she come down to Maldon early in the war with her mother, two sisters and a family friend. As they were bombed out of several houses in London throughout the war, Patricia can't remember where they were living when they came to Maldon, but she has reason to remember the journey quite vividly.

" We came down in an open-backed truck with our household things on the back. On route we were actually machine-gunned by a German pilot. What stands out in my mind was the sound of it because all the pots and pans were pinging as the bullets hit them. Mum was upset, she said, 'we've come down here to get away from all this!'"

Luckily nobody was hurt. Patricia was too young to be very scared. She was aware of why they were moving but saw it as more as an adventure, or a long holiday, especially as she had her mother with her. She started her first school in Maldon and remembers the school bus picking her up.

They all stayed in a house called the White House which was on Maldon or Mundon Road on the edge of town, and her mother worked in the Women's Land Army. The house was owned by a family who were in the theatre. It was a big rambling house and great fun for the youngsters.

"I remember up in the loft there were boxes of costumes; beautiful clothes with sequins and feathers. We used to creep up there and play at dressing up which was great fun, but we got told off if we were caught trying them on."

There were soldiers billeted nearby and when they marched past with their boots crunching on the gravel path, the children were bundled into the giant chimney breast to hide because her mother was worried they might be German soldiers. She remembers another occasion when a German pilot landed in the field at the back of the house.

"He landed the aeroplane and stood in the field combing his hair. He was very young. I was told later that he said he'd landed and given himself up because he didn't want to drop bombs on anyone."

Eventually they had to leave the house, which Patricia believes was requisitioned for the Army. They returned to London and she was eventually re-evacuated with her older sister to Lancashire, returning just in time to experience the doodlebugs.

She later married and had four daughters and 10 grandchildren. She has returned to Maldon many times since the war, bringing her girls when they were younger, and introducing them to familiar sights.

The following extract from the Civil Defence War Diary may be referring to the aeroplane which Patricia remembers landing:

```
DATE.        TIME.      PLACE.       MISSILE.        CASUALTIES.
3/9/40.      10.38.     Stud Farm    Messerchmitt    1.
                        Mundon.      110.

REMARKS.

Plane intact but for broken undercarriage. Pilot
uninjured - handed over to Military. Gunner severely
wounded - conveyed to St. Peter's Hospital.
```

"I remember very well the bus from Witham with the gas tank behind."

Mr William (Billy) T Goddard, Keynsham, Bristol – compiled from a letter and an interview

I read with interest your letter in the "Prime of Life" regarding Maldon and Heybridge during the war.

I was evacuated to Witham 1941 - 1945 but was fortunate to have my grandparents living at Heybridge – Mr and Mrs T Courtney. They lived at Colchester Road as it was then, which was a cul-de-sac off the main road. I spent all my holidays with them during the school period. I remember very well the bus from Witham with the gas tank behind. The bus went through Wickham Bishops. I do not remember having to show a pass to go in and out of the district but do remember that towards the end of the war buses were commandeered by the Army. The soldiers would just get on a bus and say they needed it. The bus would finish its journey then be driven off by the soldiers.

When the air raids were on I remember I used to go with my grandparents over to the Flat Tops where they used to play cards, at times it was very frightening. The Flat Tops were at the end of their garden. The Flat Tops were terraced square shape bungalows, probably still there. The road to them off the Colchester Road was somewhere near the hospital. I remember the street shop on the corner where the man who owned it made cone shaped bags for the sweets. I played in all the fields round about, now housing estates. At the end of their road were fields and a wood, I believe it was called Bluebell Wood. I'm not too sure but a German plane came down either in or near it.

I have great memories of Maldon "Prom" as it used to be known, playing in the sand and water at the lake, also the boating lake. I am aware that people will have far more memories than me but I was so thrilled to read about it in this part of the country I just had to write something.

I was born in London that is how I became an evacuee. My mother was a Maldon – Heybridge woman. I still have relations there.

"Everyone was splattered in mud."

Interview with Mr Kenneth Arthur Long, Bexhill On Sea, East Sussex

Kenneth was officially evacuated from Bexhill-on-Sea to Wiltshire, but went home again quite soon. In the middle of the Battle of Britain, in 1940, his parents decided it would be a good idea to evacuate as a family to stay with his grandmother in Beeleigh Road, Maldon. He was eight years old and he came with his 11 year old sister and their mother. His father joined them two years later.

Kenneth went to All Saints School, then went on to Maldon Grammar School for two years; he finally went home when he was 13.

"Maldon was marvellous. I still consider Maldon my 'home town' and often come back to visit my cousins in Heybridge. I remember playing on Hillyfields, on top of the railway bridge, and going rowing on the river. I spent a lot of time at Promenade Park. I was on the promenade one day, at the weekend probably, because it was crowded, and a doodlebug came down and landed in the mud opposite where I was standing. Everyone was splattered in mud. I also remember the secondary school being machine-gunned."

After the war he went back to Hastings Grammar School. He became a dental mechanic, went on to became an RAF Radar Mechanic, and then went into electronics. He finally went to work at the Royal Greenwich Observatory.

"We even spent some lessons sitting in the shelter with our gas masks on and we talked in sign language."

Mrs Ivy Coker (Née Fenton), Great Totham, Essex – compiled from an interview and a letter

In 1938 Ivy was warned that she may have to be evacuated with her school. At that time she went to visit her father's cousins in Heybridge; who said that if they were going to be evacuated they should go to stay with them. So on 3rd September 1939 she came down in a taxi from Stratford, London, with her mum and sister, to stay at Springfield Cottages, Heybridge. Ivy was 11 years old and her sister was three. War was actually declared as they travelled down.

When they arrived the schools were still on holiday.

"It was probably for the blackberry picking holiday. School holidays started in mid June to mid July for four weeks, and then we had the first two weeks in September; instead of the six week July to September holiday. All the children used to help strawberry picking in the first holiday and then with blackberry picking in September.

When school finally started Ivy went to Maldon Secondary School for Girls.

"When they arrived we were all sat down in the hall while they decided what to do with us. We were all grouped according to age and spent several days in the main hall where we were given tests and placed into classes. I was lucky to be in the same class as a relative the same age at the school. I remember there were some Dr Barnardos girls from Woodford at the school. Because I was already familiar with Maldon and had relatives there nothing was really strange, although I was very aware of why we were being evacuated."

"If a siren went as we were walking to school all the children were to go into the nearest shelter and stay there until the all-clear. At school they had built blast walls in the corridor to use as the shelter. We spent quite a long time in the corridor, sitting on coconut matting. An air raid warning wasn't an excuse to stop work – we had to do lessons! We even spent some lessons sitting in the shelter with our gas masks on and we talked in sign language."

Several boys from Wanstead High School were billeted near where Ivy stayed.

They used to play cricket together and Ivy recalls that everyone got on well. But she stayed long after Wanstead group left; to finish her schooling at Maldon.

In her spare time Ivy walked a lot and played in Promenade Park. She remembers being in the park when a plane was shot down. She also went swimming at Mill Beach where there was a raft in the water.

"I had my bike with me, but it was difficult to ride at night because I had to have shields over the bicycle lamps to act as blackouts to keep the beam of light down. On one occasion I nearly rode straight into a black cow which had wandered into the road and didn't show up in the dim light!"

Another memorable occasion was when Maldon School was machine-gunned.

"I was in the waiting room at the bus station in Maldon when the senior school was machine-gunned. It was in the morning. I didn't see anything but heard it all and found out later that it was the school they were aiming at. The pilot had mistaken it for a Military Hospital."

Ivy's mother and sister went back in November 1939, then returned to Heybridge when the Blitz started. (They were made homeless a few months later when their house was destroyed by bombs dropping nearby.) Ivy was quite philosophical about the separation although she was homesick.

"In May 1942 we had a home at last and I returned there when I left school in July 1942. But we had to leave that house and we returned to Heybridge in the November never to go back to the city."

In later years Ivy returned to live in the district with her family.

An Essex farm worker painting stripes on a herd of black cows to make sure they will be visible to motorists at night.

Photograph – Imperial War Museum

"The shock when we hit the freezing cold water knocked the breath completely out of our bodies."

Letter from Mr Anthony E Williams, Billericay, Essex

In response to a notice in a recent issue of the "ARP 050 Reporter" paper, you may be interested to hear my recollections of the time.

Whilst I was not exactly evacuated to the area, as a young boy of nearly 12 years of age, I was on holiday with my mother, staying with a family at Heybridge Basin when war was declared on September 3rd 1939. The area was well known to us as my father and I used to go there nearly every Sunday during the season to fish in the Chelmer at Heybridge. My father was down for the week-end at the time and he decided that the best thing to do for the time being was for my mother and me to stay there until things became more clear as to what was going to happen. We continued to stay with the same family, the father was a fisherman with his own boat and there were two boys, one about my age and one slightly older.

We boys continued with our normal life, playing, fishing, swimming, walking etc., with occasional trips into Maldon, with my father visiting at week-ends when he could get down. We used to swim a lot off the sea wall near the lock gates into the River Blackwater going out to the boys' father's boat when it was there. When the tide was in, the water was about 20/30 feet deep and the visitors were quite amused watching us boys run as fast as we could and jump off the sea wall into the water. The time went on and nothing much was going on, I can't remember what happened about schooling at the time, as it was the early years of the war things were a bit chaotic and not very well organised. It was the days of the "phoney war" as they called it.

My mother and I eventually returned to our home in Chadwell Heath, Essex towards the end of November '39.

My most vivid memory of my time spent at Heybridge during that time was of one day early in November when us boys decided to go for a swim, it was pretty chilly as you can guess, but we did our usual run off the wall and jumped out into the water as far as we could, the shock when we hit the freezing cold water knocked the breath completely out of our bodies and we all had quite a struggle to make it back to the wall and clamber out. It may not be much but it has remained in my memory ever since and I look back with some pleasure at the time I spent in Heybridge Basin all those years ago.

Regretfully I have no photographs of those days and I can't even remember the name of the family we stayed with but I can still see them in my minds eye to this day.

"For years all my clothes were made out of that yellow silk."

Interview with Mrs Joyce Chivell (Née Rees), Heybridge, Essex

Joyce was only three years old when she was evacuated with her mother and her six year old twin brothers, from Leytonstone in East London. They went to Roundbush Road in Purleigh and stayed in a rented farm cottage. Her grandmother and aunt also came down from London during the war, and her aunt was in the ATS (Auxiliary Territorial Service). Her father joined them for a short time then went back to London on his motor bike. He was in the ARP (Air Raid Precautions) at the beginning of war and had a butchers shop in the East End. Later he was called up and Joyce didn't see him for another six years.

Joyce's mother helped on the farm, joined by a Women's Land Army girl who was staying in Purleigh. She was very resourceful, keeping 50 chickens and growing her own food. They were only allowed to keep a small amount of eggs and chickens to eat themselves because they were rationed; the rest went for distribution. At harvest time everyone helped, including the children. Her mother also bred rabbits for food and the skins were made into items like gloves and scarves for soldiers.

Her mother also helped out with the war effort by making parachutes. Tiny as Joyce was, she was not too young to help.

"I remember the parachutes were made out of yellow silk. I helped by sewing the holes where the ropes went through, which was quite a responsible job when you think about it. After the war Mum had yards of silk left over and for years all my clothes were made out of that yellow silk. I've still got the sewing machine Mum used. We had blackout curtains made out of old blankets. We only had oil lamps – no electricity – and a kitchen range. We also had a tin bath; boiling water for it in a copper."

Joyce's mother was not only resourceful, at just 5' 2" she could also be fierce if required. While her husband was at war his tools and parts of his motorbike were "requisitioned" by the Army. But Joyce's mum wasn't having that as she knew he would need them when he returned, so she told them to bring them all back – and they were returned.

As she was so young Joyce was not really aware of the war or why they had moved to the country, but she can remember hearing bombers go over, and regularly hearing the siren and being frightened of air raids. On one occasion a bomb dropped a mile away and the ceiling came down. She used to sleep on a mattress under a table at night with her brothers.

When Joyce was old enough she went to Purleigh Village School, where she remembers the blackout curtains and having to carry their gas masks with them all the time.

On the whole, Joyce has happy memories of those years, except for her father being away. He sent a tea chest of goodies from Italy with chocolate and two tins of boiled sweets, one of which she took in to school. But it didn't make up for him not being there.

"It must have been very hard for Mum being on her own for all those years bringing up a family and not knowing what happened to my father. Dad used to look after Montgomery's jeep as a mechanic. He actually went missing in Greece at one stage during the war which must have been a terrible worry to her. He didn't come home until about two years after the war, by which time we hadn't seen him for over six years. I didn't recognise him when he came home. When he came back he arrived at about six in the morning. He got a lift from the postman who was beeping his horn waking everyone."

At the end of the war the family decided to stay in the cottage. Her father started a small garage and cycle shop then eventually went back to butchery.

Joyce now lives in Heybridge. She has been married 36 years and has four daughters and eight grandchildren.

"My mother described her time at Cold Norton as 'hard'."

Compiled from letters from Mrs Lynda Rooke (Née Cawte), Rayleigh, Essex

I refer to a recent article which appeared in the "Evening Echo".

My mother originally came from the Tidal Basin, at Canning Town but shortly after the birth of her second child (in fact, on her way home from hospital with the new baby) her house was completely demolished in an air raid. She went to stay with her mother nearby and then the whole family (consisting of my grandmother, two aunts, my mum, my brother Ken and sister Barbara) went to Kent to work in the hop fields. As my mother had the children to look after she stayed in the hut all day whilst the rest of the family worked in the fields. There were four adults and two children in the hut and everyone slept on straw beds. My father remained in London and after six weeks he was able to find alternative accommodation in Cold Norton, where my mother spent the next eight years.

Initially, my grandmother and aunts also shared the house at Cold Norton but after two years they moved out.

Whilst my mother was at Cold Norton she had another two children, Maureen and June. Money was scarce and my father could only come home at weekends. He was working for the railways in London.

My mother described her time at Cold Norton as "hard". She was very near starvation level at times as my father could not send much money and, of course, everything was rationed.

On one occasion she was desperate because the coalman was due to call and she still hadn't paid for the previous delivery. He had already warned her that he could not leave any more coal until his bill was paid and Mum didn't have a brass farthing. Luckily my gran arrived minutes before the coalman and she was able to settle the bill. So that night, the family was warm at least even though everyone was hungry!

I'm sure my mother can recall much more heart-rending stories but I was one of the lucky ones born after the war.

Eventually, they moved from Cold Norton to Chingford where the family settled for the next 30 years. Unfortunately my father died during that time, leaving my mother to bring up a young family on her own.

My mother now lives at Witham, near my sister Maureen who was born at the Cold Norton house in 1944.

"Dad painted the light bulbs with black paint until the curtains were ready and when he switched the light on we couldn't see a thing."

Letter from Mrs Pamela Makepeace (Née Morlidge), Hove, Sussex

I can recall staying with my grandmother (my grandfather was killed in the first world war) and my aunt (she taught science at Maldon Grammar School) on hundreds of occasions and we had some lovely family holidays there. In fact in September 1939 I was there with my parents for such a holiday and we happened to be on Maldon "Front" buying ice creams from a kiosk there and listened to Chamberlain's speech. When you're only eight you can't understand all the fuss so few words caused among the grown ups, as on the way home everyone seemed unable to talk of anything else.

I know we went out to buy very heavy curtain material which my mother made up on the sewing machine as every window had to be blacked out, not even a tiny chink of light showing. We did have a laugh when Dad painted the light bulbs with black paint until the curtains were ready and when he switched the light on we couldn't see a thing and he had to scratch some of the paint off to get a glimmer.

We chased everywhere to get my cousin, who was also on holiday with us, to get him a special gas mask as he was only five months old and it was like the bubble in a bubble car and you put the baby right in it. It was a bit panicky for his parents as the official supply had run out due to such a heavy demand, anyway we managed to get one in the end.

Before we were due to go back home to London there were lots of whispered conversations amongst the grown-ups and then I was told that as raids and invasions were likely Mum and Dad had decided to leave me with Nanny and Aunty as, compared to London, Maldon had been declared a "safe area" so I became an evacuee!

When the new term started, as we lived in London Road, I went to the school near the fire station which I enjoyed very much but it was so much smaller than my London school but very cosy. I can also remember walking up to Keebles Farm (near the cemetery) for odds and ends. Some evenings my grandmother would take me to the pictures straight from school (I expect my aunt wanted some peace to do her marking, as she brought piles of school books home every night) and when we came home it was pitch black and we used to have great fun trying to dodge the doorsteps on the pavement in the dark, nanny was often tripping up.

My aunt had a car and she got petrol coupons and we'd have trips out, sometimes local and we also went for weekends to visit my parents as, all those air raids hadn't materialised.

After a couple of months or so my aunt had two official evacuees billeted on us and these were two boys. Unfortunately I can't remember where they came from. One day they were practising their fencing in the lounge and smashed the glass lampshade, my aunt wasn't very pleased but nanny just said "boys will be boys", I made myself scarce.

I'd been living in Maldon for about nine months when the authorities decided it wasn't a "safe place" anymore, as they'd had air raids and bombs etc., so it was decided I'd return to my parents in London. As soon as I got to London the Blitz started, we stayed in London all through the war and were bombed out of our house in the height of the Blitz.

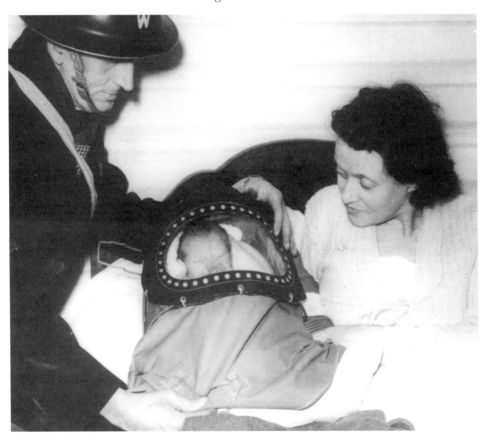

A new born baby inside a special baby's respirator at the start of the war.

Photograph – Imperial War Museum

"We had to transfer to buses to get round the craters in the main line."

Compiled from a letter on tape from Ramon Harold Holland, Harpenden, Herts

These are my memories of staying with my aunt and uncle in Maldon during the war years. Their names were Mr and Mrs Wharton, they lived at Park Drive. I stayed there for nine months and had to go to school there. I know that my Uncle Charlie worked for Sadds and during the first part of the war he helped to build the first wooden MTBs (Motor Torpedo Boats) and landing craft ready for the invasion in 1944.

I remember seeing cars with gas bags in the early part of the war and there used to be buses pulling a mobile furnace at the back which supplied them with gas for power to save petrol.

There's one little incident when we were coming down from Liverpool Street on the train. The line was bombed and we had to transfer to buses to get round the craters in the main line. By the time we got to Witham and transferred to the single track line to Maldon and arrived in Maldon, it was about midnight. It was winter time and so you can imagine it was pitch black. We walked from the station up through the park to get to Park Drive. When we arrived at the gates they were unfortunately locked, so my mother and myself – I was about eight or nine years old and she was about 16 to 17 stone in those days – climbed over these gates. My mother ripped her dress. But the funny point about it is that when we woke up in the morning, we looked out and all the railings had been taken down, apart from the gates, the ornate gates, so we could have walked round the side anywhere along the length of Park Drive without climbing over anything. It's always been a laughing joke within the family about the sight of mother climbing over those gates.

There was another small incident I remember. We were at the station, either arriving or going away, and there was a convoy of troops came down Market Hill out of Maldon. The train used to stand across the level crossing, so they couldn't open the gates until it left, so the outriders went underneath the small bridge at the side and the convoy tried to follow through. The leading truck in the convoy had an officer facing back, who was signalling the convoy to follow him underneath the railway, and of course he didn't see the low bridge and he was killed. I remember seeing that, he knocked his head on the low bridge and it killed him outright.

There was a little shop in the High Street, at the lower end of the High Street, which was called The Rock Shop and I can't remember the name of the couple that ran it, but it was an elderly couple, and if you took your sugar there they would turn it into rock for you. This was a great thing to have during the war because there were hardly any sweets about. We used to save up our sugar ration as much as we could and get our rock made when we used to go down there visiting.

At the latter end of the war I remember watching the doodlebugs flying over and there was one struck the chimney on one of the houses right at the top of the town, and the unfortunate part about it is that the house that it struck was a friend of my cousin. My cousin used to work in the hospital and lived in, and she'd changed shifts. The person she'd changed with was in the house when this doodlebug struck. She was killed. A very unfortunate change of shift, I'm afraid.

My cousin, Olga and I were speaking recently about memories of Maldon. She used to work for Sadds in the offices. She related a little story about when she was in the offices there and they *(a German aeroplane – editor)* came and machine-gunned Sadds. She was just coming out the door, one of the last out, and dived back inside for safety. My Uncle Charlie, who was stone deaf, didn't know what was going on and they managed to tell him that somebody had been machine-gunned in this raid, and he thought she'd been killed, but of course when he saw her alive he was very thankful.

There was a family called Holland that lived just off of Park Drive. He was a fisherman and I got very friendly with his son, because his surname was the same as mine, I can't remember his Christian name. He was telling me that his father was involved in the evacuation at Dunkirk and went and took his little fishing boat over to help the rescue in Dunkirk so it was quite an experience I should think. We did actually go fishing once, I don't think we were supposed to, but we had a pleasant day just in the estuary to do a bit of fishing.

Another thing I remember is the big Thames sailing barges used to come and unload at Sadds with brick red canvass sails. They were a terrific sight and they had big bat-shaped stabilisers on the side. I remember my uncle telling me that these were used as paddles when there was calm and there was no wind. I believed that for quite some time, before I found out that what they really were for was to stabilise when they were out into the ocean going round into the Thames.

Some parts of the "Prom" were off-limits during the war of course; and my aunt and uncle owned a dog called Cocoa, a brick red, very dark, red setter. Of course one young boy and a dog could get into these sort of areas because the soldiers used to make friends with the dog and the boys, and we used to go in. I know we weren't supposed to be there, but there again what boy wouldn't like to go and see something that's forbidden, especially in those years?

The following extract from the Civil Defence War Diary is probably the incident Ramon refers to at the railway bridge:

```
DATE.          TIME.       PLACE.         CASUALTIES.
31/8/42        14.00.      Fullbridge.    3(1 fatal)

REMARKS.
3 ton R.A.F. lorry from 71, Maintenance Unit, R.A.F.
Depot, Slough, was passing under L.N.E.R. Bridge when
top of lorry struck span of bridge. 3 casualties -
1 died later in hospital.
```

Men at work removing the railings fr
Lord Beaverbrook's house, to provid
iron for the war effort in 1941.

Photograph – Imperial War Museum

OTHER EVACUEES

This section records the memories of other evacuees who were sent to the district, including boys who were evacuated with the LCC Training Ship Exmouth. The first letter refers to the questionnaire, which was sent out to some of the respondents to the appeal for memories.

"Coming along Wantz Road at about 40 feet, was a German aircraft. It was firing all machine-guns."

Letter from David William Thomas, Oakham, Rutland

PART 1

I was initially evacuated from London to Maidenhead, but the family I was billeted with decided to move to the coast where they had some friends of long standing. So we went firstly to Goldhanger, a small village on the River Blackwater. After a few months there we moved to a summer-type chalet at Mill Beach.

After a further few months in the chalet we moved to "The Limes", Hall Road, Heybridge. During all this frenzied moving my two sisters were still at Maidenhead, staying with the same foster parents for the rest of their evacuation.

During my stay in Essex I was not visited by my parents as they were both in the Services. My father was an instructor in the RAF down in Wiltshire, and my mother was in the WRNS as a censor, (due to her ability to speak Welsh fluently).

I don't remember how we travelled to Essex from Maidenhead, although I can only imagine it was by rail, via London. During my stay in the area my school was at Wantz Road, in Maldon. I am not too sure of the duration of my stay in the area. I have tried to work out the year that I returned to London, it was possibly 1943.

After my return to London I won a scholarship to an art school in Hammersmith, London. Shortly after commencing my studies at that school Hitler's V2 assault on London commenced, I was evacuated again, this time to Wiltshire. Due to lack of initiative and general apathy, I did not keep in touch with anyone in Essex, although I did make a fleeting visit whilst in the RAF (which was to become my career for the next 22 years).

I took my wife to the district about 15 years ago, this was purely on a sightseeing trip.

PART 2.

Yes! I did understand why I was evacuated. I had lived in London throughout the Blitz, quite an unpleasant experience. Being evacuated was another adventure as far as I was concerned, although some people I knew were terribly upset at being away from their parents and homes, I had already travelled quite a lot in my young life.

The lady I was evacuated/fostered with was a Mrs Skelton, her husband was in some strange job, (I always though he was a SPY!!)

I generally enjoyed going to school at Maldon, there were some wonderful teachers.....Mrs Keeble, (I had a schoolboy crush on her!).....Mr Tanner and Mr Clouten, (an unbelievable combination of names)....Mr Horner, the headmaster, very stern but very fair...and last, but most certainly not least, my favourite, Mr Green. He impressed me with his ability to pronounce foreign words/names, the Dutch words and places in "Moonfleet" for example. Before school each day I did a paper round with Glyn Phillips, and when we were paid at the end of the week we used to walk down the hill in Maldon to Pettitts, the bakers and buy such things as were available, (rationing was in force then, of course).

The school bus was a source of great amusement to all the schoolchildren. It was powered by GAS! It had a strange two wheeled trailer into which was built a stove-like fire. The plan was that the fire would burn coal which, in turn, would give off gas. This gas was fed into a huge balloon situated on the roof of the bus. Invariably the supply of gas would run out somewhere on the trip into Maldon. The most common point was about a third of the way up Market Hill. At this point we all had to alight from the bus and walk up the remaining portion of the hill. Sometimes the bus would catch us up, but more often than not we were obliged to walk the rest of the way to school.

On one of these journeys Glyn Phillips and I were walking along Wantz Road when we heard a very loud roaring of engines. Coming along Wantz Road at about 40 feet high, was a German aircraft. It was firing all machine-guns. This aircraft had machine-gunned the school – all the blast walls were pock-marked where they had been hit.

As it flew overhead I could make out members of the crew, I could see every detail, it was so close! I was riveted, I was fascinated! Off it went, up Wantz Road, over the town. I heard that it had done some damage to John Sadds' wood yard. I looked for Glyn after this event. He had performed a vertical leap into an adjacent garden and was sheltering behind a convenient privet hedge!! I was a very keen aircraft spotter in those days. I identified the aircraft as a Ju.88.

I joined the RAF in 1947 as an aircraft apprentice, training for three years at Cranwell on radar and wireless. After my 22 years service I joined Marconi Radar Defence Systems at Leicester. I was a senior field engineer employed as company service representative at Goonhilly Ground Station, (remember Telstar?) My next tour was in Singapore. I was accepted for a post in Saudi Arabia, (British Aerospace) and later took up a post in Brunei. I left Brunei in February 1993 and returned to the UK to take up a well earned early retirement!!!

Due to the various geographical locations relating to my employment my wife and I have been able to travel extensively and yet we both say that there is no better place to be than here at home in Britain.

"In the panic my small brother left one wellington stuck in the mud."

Compiled from letters from Mrs E Bunyan (Née Amiss), Islington, London N1

I enclose a copy of a letter to my mother dated 1938 about evacuation which I am sure you will find of interest. However I regret that I know very little about Mr Clark of Stow Maries for I believe we only stayed with him for a short time pre-war when I was about six or seven and then my mother returned to her home in London.

All I can remember is Mr Clark worked on a farm and had a daughter. The only other memory that I have of Mr Clark is that he gave me an apple when I was in the school playground, and he was ploughing in the field just behind, during the early part of the war when we were evacuated there.

When the war did start, unfortunately Mrs Browning could only take one child, so rather than separate us my mother took my brother Richard then aged six, and myself, aged nine, to South Woodham Ferrers to stay with an elderly couple.

We stayed at King Edward Road (which wasn't exactly a road but more like a muddy track in inclement weather). However the area was then very rural with fields to the rear and fields and the railway line in front. We sometimes collected milk from a farm in a rear field, in a small hand-type churn. The bungalow was a small timber dwelling with a bucket-toilet shed in the back garden.

We occasionally walked to the river which could be crossed on foot at low tide though naturally extremely muddy. I vaguely remember being with my small brother on a hillock, about early 1940, when we saw two planes firing at each other and could quite clearly see the puffs of smoke. The German plane was shot down elsewhere. We ran down the hill and in the panic my small brother left one wellington stuck in the mud at the field-gate and ran the rest of the way in only one boot.

The reason we were taken back to Woodham Ferrers was that my mother had been a temporary housekeeper to a farmer there when she had left London for a break, after my father and her two other children had died quite close together in the mid 1930's.

We also had an aunt who had run the local general shop which in those days seemed to sell practically everything as far as I can recall. Also there was a butcher's shop opposite it called Franklins, which name I assimilated because of the then topical song "Mr Franklin D Roosevelt Jones".

I was extremely homesick and eventually persuaded my mother to fetch us back to London, also the elderly couple intended to move nearer their family at Michaelmas. We were at Woodham about eight months, though I was more settled upon our return to London in spite of the bombing and the Blitz.

To me Essex seemed a million miles away as I then hadn't much idea where it was in relation to London. Ironically it has now become a commuter region, and I have since lived in the Far East.

At the time we felt rather isolated so did not realise that there were other children evacuated to East Anglia, or more particularly, to Essex, for at our age then, we knew only London.

I trust that these recollections may help with the information you are seeking. I didn't think that I'd be part of history! Incidentally, my mother was born at the turn of the century (1900 – the Boer War) and has lived through two World Wars. She is the same age as the Queen Mother.

During the war we lived in Camden Passage which has now become a trendy antique tourist venue.

Copy Of Letter Referred To Above.

30/9/38

Dear Mrs Amiss

Your letter to hand for which we thank you for your good wishes and pleased to say the new shop is doing all right. Regarding the children, I sincerely hope all this evacuation will not be necessary & personally I don't think it will but as you say should the worst come you will be able to rely on us not to turn them down. We have had the local man round for us to book up for two children and I told him I have practically fixed up with you if necessary. The news this morning is very encouraging & seems to have raised strong hopes of peace in everybody so don't worry old dear. By the way I have seen Mr Clark & he says he will be pleased to have you & the children with him for a while, & will you please write to him, his address is – Salcotes Farm, Stow Marie, Essex. He has asked me for your address a long time but I could not think of it so don't forget to write him. Must close now, wishing you all we wish ourselves & hoping you will have no use for your gas mask.
We are
Yours sincerely

Mr & Mrs Browning

"I always intended to return and see if things have changed."

Letter from Mrs Barbara Jones (Née Redgewell), Twickenham, Middlesex

I was evacuated to Goldhanger for about three years. I was born in 1940 and taken by my mother to stay with a great aunt and uncle. I continued going back every year until about 1954 and I believe I may still have distant relatives in the area. My maternal grandfather came from the area of Goldhanger.

I heard a lot about my early life from my mother, but have many memories of later years. It never seemed to change much. I used to go to a marina in Maldon to paddle and Mill Beach where there were caravans. I always intended to return and see if things have changed. I will one day.

"One amusing incident ... involved Lord Haw Haw claiming to have sunk the TS Exmouth, not knowing it was a brick building. "

Compiled from letters from William G West and Dennis Stevens, Newton Abbot, Devon

Regarding your letter in the "News of the World", were you aware that all the boys of the LCC Training Ship Exmouth, were evacuated to Burnham-on-Crouch at the outbreak of war? We were based at the Royal Corinthian Yacht Club. We were only at Burnham-on-Crouch for a few months before moving to Lydney in Gloucestershire in June 1940.

TS Exmouth was an LCC Training Ship moored off Grays in Essex. Boys were trained for entry into the Royal and Merchant Navies, it was later amalgamated with The London Nautical School.

Boys from TS Exmouth were among the very first evacuees in the country. It might even have been a couple of days prior to the declaration of war that the Exmouth was evacuated, but certainly in September 1939. The ship was towed to Scotland somewhere and used as a base ship for submarines, later broken up. Boys were evacuated to Burnham-on-Crouch, using local homes for billets for sleeping only. Meals and instruction in seamanship and schooling were carried out in the Royal Corinthian Yacht Club.

I personally had already been accepted for the Exmouth but joined directly at Burnham-on-Crouch from County Hall. I was 13 at the time. I joined in September 1939 but left in early 1941 to join HMS St George in the Isle of Man.

I have a friend who lives a few doors away from me here in Devon who joined from the ship, Dennis Stevens.

One amusing incident at Burnham-on-Crouch involved Lord Haw Haw claiming to have sunk the TS Exmouth, not knowing it was a brick building.

Another thing Dennis and I can recall was the ship's band playing to the locals in our make shift parade ground at the Royal Corinthian Yacht Club. Dennis was a drummer. We were both South Londoners.

I went on to serve in HMS London on the Russian convoy run in 1942 and then on to the Far East for the remainder of the war. Dennis Stevens served much the same but on Destroyers. He was a Seaman Boy, I a Signal Boy. We have never been back to Burnham-on-Crouch. We do however retain it in our memories.

Further to previous correspondence I attach a copy of a photo taken of TS Exmouth boys taken at Burnham-on-Crouch Station, when leaving for Lydney in June 1940. All of those boys went to sea as boys in either the Royal or Merchant Navies.

EXMOUTH BOYS WELCOMED TO BURNHAM

An interesting little ceremony took place on Friday, when the boys of the training ship Exmouth received a welcome to the Royal Corinthian Clubhouse, Burnham, which has been placed at their disposal. The boys, to the number of about 250, were drawn up in the space between the Clubhouse and the Dormy House, and were addressed by Commodore W. F. R. Smithwick, captain-superintendent of the Exmouth, who expressed thanks for the kindness and hospitality of the committee of the club, who had granted the boys the use of the Clubhouse. He also thanked the inhabitants of Burnham for the cordial welcome they had given the boys, and said he hoped that, whether the stay of the boys was long or short, that good feeling would not be impaired.

The flag of the Royal Corinthian Club was then lowered from the flagstaff, and, amid cheers, the flag of the Exmouth was hoisted.

Col. Moore, secretary of the Royal Corinthian Club, said it was his duty, on behalf of the Commodore, flag officers, and members of the club, to hand over their premises to the officers and boys of the Exmouth, and to place them in their keeping, to guard and respect as they did their old ship.

" I think it is as well," Col. Moore continued, ' for you to know a little of the history of this club. Our President is H.R.H. the Duke of Kent, our Admiral is H.M. King Christian X. of Denmark, and the club was founded in 1872, 67 years ago. The primary object of this club has always been the encouragement of sailing, and many well-known amateur sailors are among our members, including Mr. Sopwith, Mr. Fairey, Sir William Burton and Mr. Boardman, who won the gold medal at the last Olympic Games. When Endeavour went to America in 1934, her crew was entirely composed of Corinthians. The club had the honour of training the Royal Navy team which defeated all nations at Kiel last month. Many members gave their lives and services during the last war, and many are serving in the forces to-day. During your stay here, which I hope will be a happy one, you will have a two-fold duty: to maintain the honour of your ship and to maintain the honour of the Corinthians, and I look to you one and all to do your duty."

Three cheers were given for the club, and the boys then marched in to enjoy their first meal there.

On Sunday morning the boys, with their brass band and bugles, marched to the St. Mary's Church.

The boys have all their meals at the Royal Corinthian Club but are billeted out for sleeping. A section of the boys makes use of St. Mary's Hall for instrumental purposes, including band practices.

*Boys from the LCC Training Ship
Exmouth, waiting at Burnham-on-Crouch
station, when leaving for Lydney in
June 1940.*

"I just got in the van and drove it down the road."

Interview with Mr Roy W Whiteman, Great Totham, Essex

When Roy and his family were bombed out of their home in Canning Town, London they were evacuated to a house in Wantz Chase, Maldon. Most of the family came, including his grandmother and grandfather (Mr and Mrs Barritt), two aunts, an uncle and two cousins. His father, who was working for West Ham Council in London, travelled back every weekend by motor bike to stay with the family in Maldon.

Roy was just four years old when he was evacuated, so his first experience of school was as an evacuee, when he started school at Maldon Primary in Wantz Chase.

"Like most kids my priority was playing. I remember having a friend called Ken Cowlin. We used to play in the big car park by the Embassy cinema. There was a giant walnut tree there and we used to go and collect the nuts. As I was so young I wasn't really aware of the war. It was very pleasant being in Maldon for us children. I remember the paddle boats on the 'Prom', going to Beeleigh Abbey and blackberrying in Great Totham. My mother had a friend in Danbury so we used to go there quite often, she walked both ways, sometimes pushing me in a chair."

When he was a bit older he got into a bit of a scrape.

"There was a local dentist called Miss Donovan, who did a milk round. I used to watch her drive the milk van around and one day I decided to have a go. I just got in the van and drove it down the road. Luckily I didn't drive it into anything!"

Roy is another who remembers the school being machine-gunned. He recalled seeing the plane coming over very low and everyone in the playground running and how frightened they all were. But he thought it was a dream and didn't realise that the incident really did happen until now. He also recalls an aeroplane coming down over Purleigh.

After they had been living in Maldon a while, Roy moved with his mother and father into Butt Lane, Maldon, which relieved the congestion in Wantz Chase. His mother's twin sister, her husband and his cousin, lived nearby at 39 Washington Road, Maldon. Sadly, they were all killed when the bomb devastated Washington Road in May 1942, and his mother was heartbroken.

Later that year, or early in 1943 they returned to London to live in Upton Park. By this time the war was much more real for Roy and he can remember such pursuits as collecting shrapnel, sometimes when it was still hot.

He came back to live in the district in 1982.

"I had fond memories of the district and blackberrying in Totham, so when I came back to see a friend who was staying here I decided to return to live here myself. My son went to Plume School."

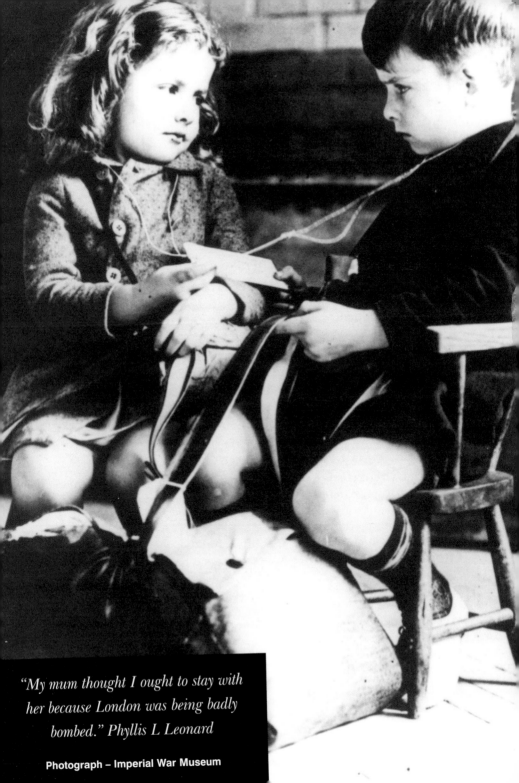

"My mum thought I ought to stay with her because London was being badly bombed." Phyllis L Leonard

Photograph – Imperial War Museum

SECTION II

OTHER MALDON MIGRANTS

·INTRODUCTION·

When the appeal for wartime memories went out, letters and phone calls flooded in from a variety of "migrants" who were not evacuees. Some of these were from people who made a fleeting visit during the war (or in a couple of cases, tried to visit but could not get in). Others were from those who came to work – as civilians, in the Forces or for the Women's Land Army. A few came from people who had moved to live in the district during the war as adults and stayed.

VISITORS TO THE DISTRICT

"My mum thought I ought to stay with her because London was being badly bombed."

Mrs Phyllis L Leonard, Sidmouth, Devon – compiled from a letter and an interview

Although I lived in East London I was never evacuated.

However my step-father, Rueben Boyce Barty, was a mercantile marine master on a small merchant ship, the MV Mallard, which was torpedoed and sunk in the English Channel in July 1940. We did not know of this fact until about 18 months later, when three members of the crew were found to have been in hospital in Cherbourg and later transferred to POW camps. One member was a Richard Caplan who I think came from Poplar, E14. I know he was the ship's cook. Because he was 70 years of age he was repatriated on a POW exchange, and it was on his return that we found out what had happened to my father.

Dick Caplan was a good friend to my father, and my mum when she used to visit the ship. His wife had been evacuated to Heybridge as she was quite elderly. I was taken for a short visit during a school holiday to have a few days break away from the bombing. She was a lovely lady and both her and my mum thought I ought to stay with her because London was being badly bombed. It was a small house in a country road and rather isolated. It seemed very rural to me even though Chingford, where I lived at the time, was not so built up then.

I didn't stay but later we heard Dick had been sent home and we lost touch with them both. I would love some news of them later in life.

"We were allowed to complete our journey to Maldon, but were to be out of town and on our return journey by 12 midnight."

Letter from Mrs Elizabeth (Betty) J Jupp (Née Glossop), Milton Keynes, Bucks

Reference your letter in the spring "Yours" I wondered if my memories would be of interest.

In 1934 my father worked for a company putting up loud speakers and broadcasting equipment for councils who were having festivals and galas during the summer.

That was the first time, we as a family, came to Maldon. Mum and Dad, my brother Don aged nine years and me, Betty, aged four years.

We stayed with a Mr and Mrs Eaton who lived at Park Drive, Maldon. Mr Eaton (Uncle Dick) was a mobile grocer and used to take his shop on wheels all round the outlying villages. Mrs Eaton (Aunty Lil) her son Geof and two daughters, Yvonne and Audrey made us so welcome, that we stayed with them every year after that and that was our summer holiday.

I can't remember exactly what year it was after the start of the war and although Dad had changed his job, we thought we would go to Maldon as usual. As money was a bit tight, Dad and my brother decided to go on their bikes, while Mum and I went by bus. We lived in Edmonton, North London, at the time and it was quite a journey, involving three buses.

When our bus from Chelmsford was some way from Maldon, the bus was stopped and the police came on board and asked if Mrs and Miss Glossop (Mum and I) were on board. We said that was us and what was the problem?

They told us that we were allowed to complete our journey to Maldon, but were to be out of town and on our return journey by 12 midnight. They had already stopped my dad and brother and told them the same thing. As you can guess, we were in a real panic, as after such a long bike ride, we didn't think Dad and Don would be in a fit state to do the return journey that day. But the police said that strangers were forbidden. Due to War Regulations.

When we arrived Dad went to see the local MP I think his name was Tom Driberg to see if we could stay over night. But he wasn't able to get permission so our holiday that year lasted only one day.

But I still have fond memories of my holidays in Maldon.

I can remember going to see a concert party which was held in a marquee on the green by the swimming pool and there used to be some spectacular fireworks displays on the river bank. They always finished with the King and Queen done in fireworks.

"Permits were not given for holiday makers."

Letter from Mrs Phyllis Upson, Warley, Brentwood, Essex

After reading your letter in the "Brentwood Weekly News" I thought you might like to know my memories of Maldon.

When I was a child we were always taken to Maldon by train for our Sunday school outing, but when the war came we were no longer allowed into Maldon for such treats.

I had an uncle and aunt who lived in Wantz Road where we spent a few holidays of two or three days but again during the war we were unable to go as visitors needed a permit to stay in Maldon and permits were not given for holiday makers. This was all very strict and secretive and I don't think I was ever told why Maldon was so special.

By the time the war was over everything had changed and I never had another holiday in Maldon and I was too grown up for Sunday school.

However we have spent several days there and last Christmas I went to the Victorian Christmas which I really did enjoy.

"Whether it was a coincidence I never found out but the female organist had fainted."

Compiled from letters from Mr Leslie K Smith, Chester-Le-Street, Co. Durham

I read your request for information in the spring edition of the "ARP 050 Reporter", and I am sending the associated which may be of help. I have no photographs unfortunately, only fond memories.

"The day war broke out......" I was living in Edmonton, London with my older brother and three older sisters, and a very young brother and baby sister, seven of us in all, a big family for Dad and Mum to cope with. Dad I believe was the only breadwinner, a labourer with no particular skills so you can imagine we were on the poverty line.

I was eight years old and would be nine in October 1939, not knowing at the time that I would be spending my birthday with a strange family. I was evacuated with two of my elder sisters to the village of White Notley, Essex, which is situated between Braintree and Witham.

I cannot recall the departure from London but remember the train journey and the waving workmen in the factories etc., along the line who probably knew more than we did what our journey was about. We had an adult with us in our carriage, a lady who could have been one of the other kid's parents, but I'm not sure, who kept us cheerful singing songs until we arrived at Braintree where we boarded a double decker bus for the journey to White Notley. We drove into the grounds of the vicarage, under the boughs of a chestnut tree and the lads near the upstairs open windows helped themselves to the conkers that were in reach.

We were then allocated to our various foster families, my sisters and I all to

different homes. I got the best of the bargain it seems as my sisters did
not stay long and soon returned home to face the bombing in London, luckily
no harm came to them and they are still around today. I was to remain with my
new family, Mr and Mrs Josling and their daughters Joan and Beryl, for almost
a year.

What a blissful happy time it was, although at the time I was unaware of it.
It was only as I grew older and began to recall the good times I had that I
began to appreciate how idyllic it was. I recall that in the winter we had a very
heavy snowfall and as I had not seen much snow in London, this was nothing
but fun although it did cause lots of headaches for traffic, not that there was a
lot around those days.

I attended the village school which had an orchard alongside the playground
and of course apple scrumping around the village in general became an
adventurous game. I also became a choir boy at the church. One of the jobs of
a choirboy was to pump the organ and there was an occasion when I was getting
a bit fed up with slowly pumping the wooden lever up and down, I gave it a
forceful down stroke and suddenly the music stopped. Whether it was a
coincidence I never found out but the female organist had fainted.

I also made myself some pocket money by delivering milk morning and
evening around the village. I did not have many customers and carried the
milk from a nearby farm in a small milk can and served this out with a half pint
ladle. I used to get in trouble because instead of serving it out myself I let the
customers help themselves and when I arrived at the final house the measure
was short. On one occasion on an icy morning, I slipped on an ice patch and
the milk went all over my short trousers etc!! and began to freeze. A passing
gentleman helped me up and kindly gave me some money to buy more milk
but I had to endure the frozen nether regions. I can recall with affection, one
elderly customer who always gave me a small bag of apples. I can still recall the
aroma of these and have not smelt anything like it since.

Whilst living down there we spent a day at Maldon and I recall travelling in
a steam train and clearly remember the riverside recreation area and the red
sailed barges. I can also recall an outdoor swimming pool. I revisited Maldon
on one occasion many years later.

My dad came to see me one day and he was in his fireman's uniform. He
was a leading fireman in the Auxiliary Fire Service and was able to find some
time away from the fires in London to visit me. I was not half proud of him.
He stayed and had a meal with us before returning to the turmoil he had left.

What appears to have been erased from my memory is when and why I
left. I cannot recall saying goodbye or thanking them or anyone else for the
hospitality and kindness they had shown me, and this troubles me now. I believe
the reason I was brought back to London was that as the bombing intensified
my parents wanted us all together in case anything drastic was to happen.

I took up employment with the Post Office in 1945 as a telegram boy and after
40 years service through the ranks retired after reaching management status.

THE WOMEN'S LAND ARMY AND THE SERVICES

"When it was my turn to take a bath in the tin bath in front of the fire, her son had to go out for a walk until I was finished."

Interview with Mrs Alice Rice (Née Miles), Leigh-On-Sea, Essex

Alice's family was bombed out of their house in Dagenham in 1940, so they came to Westcliff in Essex to live. They moved on to Leigh-on-Sea in 1942 and Alice has lived in same house ever since.

Alice was very nimble fingered as a girl and was an apprentice court dressmaker. But the war put the stop to such delicate work and the beginning of the war saw her putting her skills into the war effort, making rather less fashionable clothes for the Forces. She was working at Glanfield's factory in Benfleet making uniforms when she got her first call-up papers. Because her work was important her first call-up was deferred, but when she was 20 years old a second call-up arrived.

"I was given a choice of war work: nursing, munitions or the Women's Land Army. I wanted to join the Air Force but that choice wasn't available, so I decided to become a 'Land Girl'."

On 26 May 1943 she was sent to work for Wilkins & Sons of Tiptree, who made (and still make) the famous Tiptree jam. She travelled on the Tollesbury train which was known as the "crab and winkle" train. It was an old wooden train made out of what looked like large boxes. She was based at Tollesbury and worked for a farmer called Mr Runacles.

"He was very nice and treated me very well. I did the same job as all the others and was treated just the same. We started at 6am and did a full day's work picking all the different fruits for the jams. I enjoyed the work. My wages were about £3 a week and I believe they were paid by the Government."

"I was billeted with Mrs Large in Tollesbury and still have photograph of her and her son. I remember they didn't have a proper bathroom and on the nights that it was my turn to take a bath in the tin bath in front of the fire, her son had to go out for a walk until I was finished."

Alice recalls that at that time Tollesbury was a "banned" area and seemed very much like a war zone.

"You had to carry identity cards and would only be allowed in if you lived in the area. Husbands couldn't even come home for a visit without a pass. Inhabitants couldn't go out very easily. Right round the coast the beaches were wired off and some were mined."

Alice has very happy memories of living in Tollesbury, not least because she met her future husband, Ron, there. He was a Tollesbury boy and went to

*Ron Rice, the Tollesbury boy Alice fell in
love with and who was later to become*

school in Maldon. The 'Land Girls' mixed in very well with the locals and joined in all the local entertainment and it was at the August Bank Holiday dance at the village hall that she met Ron, just three months after arriving in the district.

"There wasn't a lot to do in Tollesbury but we made our own entertainment. The men were real gentlemen, they never took advantage. Despite the blackout we were never scared in the dark or were worried about walking home. Everyone got on well together. Ron was 18 when we met, and hadn't been called up yet. We spent our courting days walking or went to see films at the village hall."

Unfortunately the work for Wilkins & Sons dried up and Alice was due to be moved to a new billet, away from Tollesbury and her beloved Ron.

"I had only just met Ron and we were very much in love and I didn't want to be sent away, so I found myself a new post working for Mr French stooking corn and turning sheaves. But that wasn't allowed, so I got slapped wrists for finding my own billet and not following the regulations, and they didn't let me stay."

Alice was sent to Roydon to do very heavy work hedging and ditching and Ron joined the Air Force. Alice still has the green and red arm bands and badges she got for good service, as well as her billeting papers and discharge papers. Every six months she was sent a new badge and a duplicated letter thanking her for her continued effort. The very heavy work she had to do on her last placement was too much for her and at the end of 1946 her health broke down and she left the Women's Land Army. The "Land Girls" and factory workers didn't get a gratuity at end of war, only the Services got this, but Alice was sent her final certificate thanking her for all her hard work.

In 1947 Ron was discharged from the RAF and they married and enjoyed many years of happy married life before Ron's sad death a few years ago. They had two sons and Alice is now a proud grandmother and still living in Leigh-on-Sea.

Alice Miles in her Land Army uniform with her sister.

" I always say we were a forgotten Army."
Molly Goodfellow

Photograph – Imperial War Museum

WOMEN'S LAND ARMY.

ESSEX COUNTY COMMITTEE.

Tel.
Writtle 313
MS.

The Priory.
Writtle.
Chelmsford.

23 JAN 1946

Dear Miss Miles,

Herewith I have pleasure in sending you your
5th Good Service Badge which represents 30 months good
service on and for the land.

I hope you will continue to be happy and succesful
in your most essential National Service.

Yours sincerely,

E. Wakeland Smith

County Secretary.
(Mrs. E. Wakeland Smith).

Badge due on 4/12/45

WOMEN'S LAND ARMY (ENGLAND & WALES).

RELEASE CERTIFICATE.

The Women's Land Army for England and Wales acknowledges
with appreciation the services given by

Miss A.V.Miles

who has been an enrolled member for the period from

7th June, 1943 to 21st December, 1946
and has this day been granted a willing release.

Date 18/12/46.

E. Wakeland Smith

WOMEN'S LAND ARMY.

"I always say we were a forgotten Army."

Letter from Mrs Molly I Goodfellow (Née Martin), Walthamstow, London E17

Seeing your letter in the spring Issue of "Yours" about Burnham-on-Crouch, Maldon etc., reminded me of the war years, no, I was not evacuated there, but I was a "Land Girl" and me and my friend were in a hostel in Burnham, near the gas works (no longer there). It was great fun.

When the War started I was 21 years old and had to register, and chose the Women's Land Army. On August 25th 1941 I was posted to a hostel in Burnham. I was living in Saffron Walden, Essex with my parents and had never been away from home before.

I travelled to Liverpool Street where I met another girl dressed in new WLA uniform, and we joined forces, her name was Freda Deverson from Romford, Essex, going to Burnham. We have been friends ever since and she spends a few days every year with me, she now lives in Spalding, Lincs.

We arrived at Burnham Station and found the hostel near the gas works. Next morning a cattle truck arrived to take us to a war agricultural farm in Bradwell. The work consisted of weeding, hoeing (boring), hay making and I loved the harvest time. In those years the summers were very hot so we walked up a lane to a small shop to buy American cream soda, nothing tasted nicer after being in the heat.

Once we picked blackberries and an Army unit nearby made us a blackberry tart which we ate in the cattle truck going home. The meals were plain but we always had stewed apples and custard or stewed apples, semolina rice, there was always the sweet. We had a warden, one day Freda and I came in, it was wet, the warden said, "did you wipe those shoes?" Silly like we went back and wiped them after walking in.

The room with six beds was on the top floor, once a land mine dropped on Burnham near the river, we never heard a thing, another time, one of the girls went out with an Army chap billeted near the cinema, and told her he could see us dressing in the mornings, we had no curtains. We looked across to the cinema.

The only complaint was on market day when the truck smelt of cattle when it picked us up. It was a good life, healthy, tiring, but we still had enough energy to go out in the evenings making friends with the Army chaps.

That was when I started smoking on the War Memorial near the river.

After about three to four years, Freda and I moved on to Battlesbridge in private digs doing general farming.

Being a county girl of Essex, I now vote the district one of my favourites, I went back several years ago, but the magic had gone, as like most places, they get spoilt the modern way.

I always say we were a forgotten Army, we got no gratitude and are never mentioned on the Remembrance Sunday or anywhere. Still it was great and I have my memories.

Burnham-on-Crouch as it is today.
Photograph – Colloryan

"The only entertainment was a small cinema owned by the local fish and chip shop proprietor, if he had fish, it was frying, if he had no fish the cinema was open."

Letter from Mrs Mary L Jarvie, Harrogate

My first experience of Essex was being stationed in Brightlingsea at the beginning of January 1942. I was to get ready an empty house to be used as living quarters for a number of Wrens, working at the base. They were living in billets with local people and it was thought that it would be sensible for them all to be together.

When I arrived a big stove was being installed, this was also to be used to supply hot water. For the time being I and the other four girls had to manage with a small Belling electric cooker and an immersion heater for hot water; just about adequate.

At that time as well as being a naval base, there were Army squads training as commandos, not that that term had yet been thought of. They seemed to spend quite a lot of time throwing down rolls of netting and barbed wire and then learning how to walk across them. They also seemed to go up and down the creeks in small boats, doing damage to the oyster beds.

The only entertainment was a small cinema owned by the local fish and chip shop proprietor, if he had fish, it was frying, if he had no fish the cinema was open.

After 10 days the living quarters were ready and I was sent to Sheerness in Kent.

This was a very busy dockyard town, quite overwhelmed by the influx of not only the Royal Navy, but barrage balloons and anti-aircraft sites. It was extremely cold and Sheerness is the only place I have lived in where the sea froze.

At the end of April I was again on the move, back to Essex. Great Baddow. Where was this?

Take the train from Liverpool Street to Chelmsford and then take the Galleywood bus, up Beehive Lane and ask to be put off at Hampton. As the bus went up Beehive Lane, the sun came out and there seemed to be flowering trees everywhere. This certainly looked more promising than Brightlingsea.

I did not realise that I was to be there for over two years. At the first opportunity I went up to Yorkshire and collected my bicycle and with this and along with another Wren, who also liked to explore, we went as well as we could to all those lovely villages, small towns etc.

The number of Wrens there increased and we had to put up two Nissen huts and when these were full, get local people to put up Wrens. Only for sleeping, as the Wrens came to Hampton for meals. Bedding was provided and brought back weekly to go to the laundry. Without exception Great Baddow residents took us all to their hearts as also did many people in Chelmsford. If I remember there were at least two cinemas, Boots library was used by many of us and the County Library provided us with 100 books changed every three months. The WVS had a small canteen which always had a warm welcome for Service girls and the Land Army girls as well.

Crompton Parkinson used to put on a monthly gramophone record concert for us.

After the American Army and USAAF (United States of America Air Force) arrived, there were always invitations to dances in enormous huts.

We used to have very regular air raids and I was so surprised to read in "The Lady" that Maldon, Burnham, Heybridge and Bradwell were areas for children to be evacuated to, some families sent their children away. We only had Hampton as E K Cole of EKCO radio moved himself to Buckinghamshire along with his family after a bomb fell into the garden. The bomb crater stayed there for all the time I was there.

I and friends would go down along the Chelmer canal towpath to Heybridge, it saved the hill to Danbury. The Blue Boar was so good to us when we spent a night there with a sleeping out pass. I think the towpath ended at Heybridge. I never went to Burnham, again this was a very busy naval base. Bradwell Church had a narrow track through minefields and I went there by myself for some reason and was quite upset when a large dog ran across the minefield chasing a rabbit and the dog was killed by an exploding mine. This was on my way back from the church otherwise I would not have gone down.

We got to know the Rector of Danbury, Jock Hopkirk and he and his wife always gave us a great welcome. Mary was writing a biography of Queen Adelaide, wife of William IV and we used to help with the proof reading. It was not possible for this to be published until after the end of the war, as portraits etc., were stored for safety in Wales. We also met Margery Allingham, writer of so many stories set in East Anglia.

When I went back to Maldon in 1989 and stayed at the Blue Boar it still seemed unchanged as did Maldon in many ways.

It has been fun for me looking back and to remember that my mother's father came from Suffolk, perhaps that is why I was so anxious to explore and why I felt so much at home in East Anglia, and despite the anxieties and tragedies of war I look back with much affection of my years there and remember kindness from so many and lovely towns, villages and countryside.

"I had never seen such emptiness."

Letter from Mrs Helen Pearson (Née Rooke), Maidstone, Kent

I was a WAAF (Women's Auxiliary Air Force) during the last war and was stationed at Bradwell Bay, Essex. I was a teleprinter operator at the Signals Headquarters, Dundonald, Belfast where I spent two years from November 1941 to October 1943 before an exchange posting to Bradwell.

The journey by train from London to Southminster took me across such flat countryside that I began to wonder where on earth I was going. I had never seen such emptiness. There was nothing but fields with a few cows in the distance and a lonely cottage or two.

At Southminster I was met by an Airman with a lorry to take me and I expect there were others from the train (although I do not remember them) to Bradwell. I was billeted in a Nissen hut. There were three huts in a field away from the main camp.

Of the village itself I cannot remember, but I do remember having to go on church parades.

Our Signals Office was at the back of Down Hall where RAF Officers were billeted. In our off duty hours during the summer we cycled to a little cafe on the waterside. I believe it was called "The Moorings". Or we would swim in the River Blackwater. We also cycled to Tillingham a few times.

I have seen a Fighter Squadron take off at dawn as it was beginning to get light. A marvellous sight. Then I believe for a special reason some of the American planes came in. It was late evening I think, FIDO (Fog Investigation Dispersal Operation) had been lit on the runways as it was a little foggy. The pilots flew round and round waiting their turn to land. Searchlights were directed on the planes. Both occasions are something I shall never forget.

I was at Bradwell until October 1945 when my next move was to Spilsby, Lincolnshire. Only for two months then I went to Watnall, Nottinghamshire. Finally I was released from Service 7th March 1946 at Wythall, Birmingham.

The chapel of St Peter on the Wall, Bradwell-on-Sea as it is today.

"Burnham survived the buzz bombs which exploded quite near."

Letter from Mrs Audrey Davies (Née Sims), Danygraig, Swansea, Wales

I spent about 18 months at Burnham-on-Crouch in the WRNS (Women's Royal Naval Service) during the war.

I was transferred from Dartmouth to Burnham-on-Crouch after Christmas leave 1943. The whole ship was drafted to Burnham, and was re-named "HMS Matthew". I worked for the Commander and was a Writer/T (typist).

Leisure time was spent in the local cinema which changed its show twice a week and in a hall where the Women's Voluntary Service did us proud with tea, coffee and home-made cakes and sandwiches. (We never asked where the rations came from!) Saturdays we would take the local bus to Maldon for shopping and cinema.

I was billeted first of all with five other Wrens, in a guest house/tea shop owned by a Miss Last and her helper, Miss Bell. We worked in a building across the road from the guest house.

Our Mess Hall was in "The Lawns" which was a beautiful bungalow in its own grounds, and was where the Wren officers were billeted, and also the Wren stewards.

On Saturday 29th July 1944, the Ship, *(a public house – editor)* which by that time had been taken over by the Royal Marines, held a regatta on the river. The local people were very friendly, very kind and helpful.

I was later moved to another billet, with three other Wrens. The lady there was a migraine sufferer, and we always had to be very quiet when we saw her green window blinds at her bedroom window.

We loved walking along the river bank where all the racing yachts had been laid up for the duration of the war, but were occupied at some weekends by their owners.

Further up the river Creeksea was occupied by the Royal Marine personnel, and we were often invited to a dance, a concert by ENSA, or a tombola session.

Some weekends in the summer we would be able to "borrow" one of the Landing Barges (we were a Combined Ops Training Base), and after raiding the galley, and with a few sailors to help, we would picnic near Creeksea. There were a lot of oyster beds further up the river – all now unused.

Our sick bay was in another beautiful bungalow and I spent some time there with a kidney infection and jaundice. After recovery I was drafted on 29 October 1945 to HMS Westcliff.

Burnham survived the buzz bombs which exploded quite near. We used to watch them as they passed overhead, and wait for the engine to cut out, then the explosion.

I helped a friend to write a book on our Eastside of Swansea called "Memories" and it is now due to be reprinted owing to its success. I am also "written up" in a book called "Wrens at Dartmouth".

NEW ARRIVALS

Many people came to live or work in the district during the war. Here is a letter from a lady who came to work for the company which has been mentioned most often in this book – Sadds. The second letter is from Christina Foyle, whose family bought the beautiful Beeleigh Abbey during the war. Whilst Beeleigh Abbey is privately owned and not open to the public, it is still as much a landmark in Maldon today as it was during the war.

"I caused quite a stir as being the first woman to continue working for six months whilst I was pregnant."

Compiled from letters from Mrs Valerie Ketley, Marple, Cheshire

I felt I had to write to you after noticing your letter in the "ARP".

My husband was called up early in 1939 and I came to Maldon as private secretary (as we were called then) to Mr John Sadd, managing director of Sadd and Sons, and spent two happy years working there. I had been living in Essex for some years, mainly in Silver End, White Notley and Black Notley. In 1939 when my future husband was called up in August I went to stay with his parents in Silver End, where I saw the advert in the local paper for a secretary to Mr Sadd, applied and got the job.

After I was married in the October I was offered the tenancy of No. 1 Foundry Terrace, as the owner was a friend of Mr Sadd's and had moved to London for a job at one of the ministries. Foundry Terrace was built by the Ironworks for their employees. I think the cottages were built at the turn of the century and were quite typical, having three rooms downstairs and three bedrooms, no bathroom or toilet, though they did have cold water to the kitchen sink. The owner had modernised the cottage years before it was fashionable to do old cottages up. One of the smaller bedrooms was made into a bathroom, although at that time there was no flush toilet, only an outside one emptied regularly by the "Nightsoil" men.

The enclosed funny old photo was taken in front of No. 1 Foundry Terrace in 1940. I understood from the neighbours that at times the River Blackwater used to overflow on a high tide and the cottages could be flooded, though it never happened when I was there. Are there any records of this having happened?

When after 18 months I became pregnant I caused quite a stir as being the first woman to continue working for six months whilst I was pregnant. At that time such women were never expected to be seen out during daylight once the coming child 'showed'. I had to return to my parents home in Cheshire in 1941 when I was expecting my first child as it was quite impossible to live on the Army allowance.

Mr Sadd organised the first section of the LDV (Local Defence Volunteers) and I took the minutes of their first meeting.

Many of the friends I made whilst working in Maldon I have lost touch with, and as I am 80 myself I am afraid many of them have since died.

Maldon was well known then for having natural fluoride in the water which must have done me a lot of good as I still have all my own teeth.

I well remember the difficulty I had making blackout shutters for the cottage, as none of the windows were square and one side was always longer than the other.

Friends in Great Waltham have taken me down to Maldon several times in the past few years and it doesn't seem to have altered very much.

My father was the author Bardley Beswick who published several books in the 1930's under the name of Eardley Beswick and who was reasonably well known at that time.

"Many of my friends took their boats across to help get the soldiers out and, there again, many of them never returned."

Letter from Christina Foyle, Beeleigh Abbey, Maldon, Essex

I was interested in your letter to "Essex Countryside". We have been coming to Essex since we were children.

Early in the war, when things were going very badly and we were really losing it, everybody expected Germany to invade England at this particular place and many people sold their houses and moved to other parts of England. It was then that my father bought Beeleigh Abbey.

It was owned by a Mr Thomas who was in his late 80's and, owing to the terrible times, he couldn't get any help in the house, the garden was covered in weeds and he was trying to get rid of the place. He offered it to Maldon Council, but they did not want the responsibility. I called one day and thought the place had wonderful possibilities and brought my father down. He bought it on the spot for a price that would really amaze you, mainly to house his marvellous library.

It was a very sad time. I watched all the planes going over to Arnheim – most of them never returned and the evacuation of Dunkirk. Many of my friends took their boats across to help get the soldiers out and, there again, many of them never returned.

Beeleigh Abbey as it is today
Photograph – Den Phillips

A child putting kitchen waste into a wartime bin for pig food.

Photograph – Imperial War Museum

SECTION III

MALDON DISTRICT RESIDENTS

·INTRODUCTION·

This final section contains the stories of the residents of the district. These include people who took in the evacuees, people who remember going to school with the evacuees and people who have other wartime memories of the district. The book ends with a story from an evacuee who left the district for a new life in South Africa.

THE SCHOOL TEACHER

The schools in Maldon, referred to throughout this book are mostly still open, although some have changed their names over the years. What is now the Lower Plume School, in Wantz Road, Maldon, was the Maldon Secondary School – split into separate girls and boys schools. It was also known as the Council Secondary School. Maldon Grammar School, in Fambridge Road, Maldon, is now the Upper Plume and Maldon County Primary is still on the same site in Wantz Road.

"We had to take our class into the shelters and just carry on teaching."

Interview with Charles Grigg Tait, Maldon, Essex

Charles came to teach in Maldon in 1938 and many generations of pupils were taught art by him before his retirement in 1975.

At the time the evacuees arrived he worked in the Boys Secondary School. He was assistant to Mr Cloughton, the billeting officer, and went with Mr Cloughton, who had a car, to deliver the children to their foster parents .

"Most of the children came on 3rd September 1939. We were in the school hall waiting for the evacuees to arrive when we heard the announcement on the radio that war had been declared. Some came by train to Maldon Station, then were taken out to the school hall by bus. Every child had a bag with provisions, including such things as a can of corned beef and some sugar. The arrangement for who went where was pre-arranged. We were responsible for taking the children to their new homes, which were mainly in Heybridge."

"A lot of the children only stayed two or three weeks during the 'phoney war'. A lot of parents came down and took children back during this period. Some of the children found it quite difficult to fit in with country life – nowhere to go, no fish and chip shop, no youth club – children used to London life found it a bit quiet here."

"Teaching was quite difficult, the school had split days of teaching in order to cope with the extra pupils. We had air raid shelters and blackouts in school. Brick screens were built outside school and we used these areas and the boiler room as shelters. Every time there was an air raid warning we had to take our class into the shelters and just carry on teaching."

Charles was called up into the Navy in October 1940. He recalls he was called up with a group of men for jobs beginning with 'S' and after 12 weeks training learning the Morse code etc., went to Portsmouth then went out to HMS Manchester as a Signalman. He didn't come back until 1946.

"I had no choice when I was called up – you went where HM Government sent you. As soon as I was able I transferred to RADAR and was in charge of the radar sets on board a Destroyer until I was demobilised."

The daylight raids started in June 1940, by this time most of the evacuees had moved on, but it was lessons as normal for the Maldon pupils. During the war schools were staffed mainly by women and unfit men as all the men were called up into the Forces.

"The war emancipated women in teaching and other areas. Women used to lose their teaching jobs on marriage. This gave preference to male teachers as bread winners. But during the war married women had to be retained and the practice of making them leave was never resumed after the war was over."

On returning from the Navy Charles went back to the school and stayed there until he retired in 1975 at 60 years. During his time at Maldon Secondary School he taught some people who later became famous or infamous, including Commander Stockwell, a former head of the Flying Squad, a former head of the Hong Kong Police and art forger Eric Hebborn – who gives tribute to him in his autobiography.

Art is still his first love and since his retirement he has published four illustrated books on Essex churches and a book on Maldon and Heybridge.

A drawing of All Saints Church, Maldon, by Charles Grig Tait. This drawing was done in 1939, before railin were removed for their iron content.

TRIANGULAR TOWER
ALL SAINTS, MALDON.

CCRIGGTAIT
1939.

WARTIME BRADWELL-ON-SEA

"You needed a pass and a security number to get into Bradwell."

Interview with Mrs Pat Benfield, Grimscott, Cornwall

Pat remembers that Bradwell-on-Sea become a restricted zone during the war because of its proximity to the sea and the aerodrome, and because of the large number of Forces which were stationed there. Although other parts of the district became restricted zones, the security appears to have been at its tightest in Bradwell.

"You needed a pass and a security number to get into Bradwell. The soldiers set up a barrier by the Queen's Head pub on the road into the village and checked everyone as they went through."

Pat, who contacted me earlier this year to say she would like to contribute some of her memories of Bradwell during the war, tragically died soon after of a stroke. Sadly all I have on record are these few brief words, which is a cruel reminder of how important it is to record people's memories while we can. She has however, written a book about wartime Bradwell (as yet unpublished), which her husband Barrie hopes to finish and publish on her behalf.

"We had a lot of evacuees arrive at Bradwell but they were all sent back."

Compiled from two letters from Mrs Peggy Lawton (Née Rayner), Oldham, Lancashire

Reading the spring issue of "Yours" I was interested to read about Bradwell-on-Sea. I was born in Bradwell and lived at the Kings Head Hotel, until I got married. My maiden name was Rayner and I lived in the Kings Head Hotel with my parents and sister. My father and his father had the Kings Head pub for a very long time.

We had a lot of evacuees arrive at Bradwell but they were all sent back to other places as it was too near the coast and too dangerous for them. They were all brought in buses into the school and then turned back.

Quite a few people were interned during the war and they had guards at the Queens Head Hotel, stopping everyone for identification.

I can remember as a girl our front room was turned into an ARP post and as soon as their was an air raid warning given my sister and I used to go round the village on our bicycles blowing a whistle, and as soon as it was all-clear we went round ringing a bell. I met my husband at the RAF station at Bradwell in 1945, I moved away to Oldham, Lancashire, and we celebrate our Golden Wedding this year.

I have lots of memories of Bradwell during the war - all the bad times and also the good times. My sister still lives in Maldon and my nephew lives in Steeple.

Modern day Bradwell Marina at Bradwell-on-Sea

"Some of my war time memories are too indelicate for you to print."

Interview with Mrs Jeanne Robinson (Née Barron Knight), Latchingdon, Essex

The Robinson family have lived in the district since 1903. At the start of the war Jeanne lived in a maternity home in North London owned by her adoptive mother, Miss D Barron. After being bombed out of their London home in 1942 Jeanne and her mother went to their holiday cottage at Bradwell Waterside.

"It was difficult to get into the district at the time as it was a restricted zone, but we managed to get permits. I worked at Bradwell Aerodrome – which they were building it at the time – as an assistant to Mr Pickles the site manager. After six months I got a job with Ernest J Gale as a lady secretary. The company managed estates and sold houses, and held the weekly Southminster Livestock Market, which had evolved from the nationally known horse sales. Part of my job involved attending the cattle market. I was not allowed to wear trousers, I had to wear a skirt regardless of what I was doing. So it caused a bit of a stir when I went to market and leaned over the pig pens in my skirt!"

By the time she arrived in the district there were few evacuees left but there were already many Servicemen in the area.

"There were no evacuees out on the Dengie. In fact people were evacuated out of here. Security was very tight. I had to show my permit at the Queens Head every day on the bus even though I knew all the officers. You could only

Conscientious objectors attending a course in mechanised agriculture under the Ministry of Agriculture's scheme at an agricultural school in Essex.

Photograph – Imperial War Museum

go to Wickford, and you couldn't even go there without your permit. There was just one made up road into the Dengie, the other route was a track, and there were tank traps on the roads."

Being an attractive young woman, she was never short of dancing partners with so many Servicemen in the district. She remembers that the Royal Artillery and Royal Highland Light Infantry were at Bradwell, the Marines at Burnham, the Devons at Southminster and of course the RAF at the aerodrome.

She met 'Randy' Churchill when he went to Burnham, and danced with Tom Driberg, the famous writer and MP for the district, in 1942 at Bradwell. He became a lifelong friend. Jeanne, who told me, "some of my war time memories are too indelicate for you to print", won't let on about any romances, but promises all will be revealed when she publishes her own book, "Death of the Dengie Hundred", which she is currently writing.

Although she had a lot of fun, life on the Dengie at that time was quite tough and very rural. She made her own butter, bread and cheese, and grew vegetables. She had no electricity or mains water until the 1960's.

"If I wanted meat I would kill a chicken or get someone to kill a sheep. If you had more than six chickens, you had to sell eggs to the Government for distribution to others on rations."

As the cottage was at the end of the runway of the aerodrome, there was the constant danger of being bombed. She had gun emplacements at the bottom of the garden and slept with a sharpened bayonet under her bed. There were quite a few bombs, and she says the RAF built a decoy aerodrome for the Germans to target, which was disturbingly close by. Several German aeroplanes were shot down over the marshes. On one occasion a German plane landed in the marshes at the bottom of her future husband's farm. It is still there today.

"I remember two German soldiers landed on the Dengie. They may have been spies. One died on landing and the other tried to get away by cycling through Latchingdon. Although dressed like a farm worker, he had clean boots and didn't reply when someone said 'good morning' – it just didn't add up, so he was caught straight away."

Towards the end of the war they left the rented cottage and bought a place at Fambridge-Hallwood Cottage. Four children came to stay with them in Fambridge, in 1944, aged about four to 12 years.

"We heard of the four 'homeless' children through one of the councillors at Maldon Rural District Council and as the children were 'on the street' he asked Mummy to help."

She believes they may have come from a children's home and doesn't think they were evacuees so much as homeless. In any case they didn't take the money to keep them. She remembers they made the boys shorts out of the blackout curtains.

She met her husband in the Southminster Market in 1942 and got married in 1945.

"He was known as the Earl of Stamford because he was such a gentleman.

He used to come to visit me on a bike. I fell in love with him when he offered his cap to me to protect me from shrapnel."

His family bought the farm where she now lives, in 1917, and her late father-in-law, John Robinson, was a founder member of the Rural District Council in 1906, when he farmed Cliffords Althorne. She believes the farm is the only one in East Anglia which is the same as it was in 1685 and she plans to keep it that way. She says she will never leave. In fact, she plans to be buried on the farm.

She remembers some of the people who came into the district to work on the land during the war.

"There were 'Land Girls' working on some of the farms but not my husband's as he didn't approve of women doing that sort of work. He had German prisoners of war. I gave them cups of tea and they made me a pair of shoes out of old tyres. There were also Italian prisoners of war and 'Conchies', (conscientious objectors) some of whose fathers had bought local farms to keep the sons out of the Forces."

Since 1984, when her husband died, Jeanne has run the farm on her own.

THE FOSTER PARENTS

"It was a very difficult time for her because she still had relatives back in Germany."

Interview with Mrs Elizabeth Mead (Née Ruffle), Heybridge, Maldon

Elizabeth has a certificate that she is very proud of. It was presented to her grandmother, Mrs Elizabeth Ruffle, at the end of the war from the Queen, (now the Queen Mother) to thank her for taking care of evacuees. Her grandmother took around five evacuees into her home in Victoria Road, Maldon. Not an unusual act for the time – until you realise that her grandmother was German.

"My grandfather went to Germany during the First World War, where he met and fell in love with my grandmother. They came back to live in England and by the time the next war started she felt she was English and wanted to do her bit to help. It was a very difficult time for her because she still had relatives back in Germany. My father was also very patriotic and wanted to join up during the war but wasn't allowed to because he was half German."

Being German didn't affect the way Mrs Ruffle was treated in Maldon. Everyone treated her as a Maldonian and her granddaughter says she was never made to feel uncomfortable because of her nationality. She cared for a series of evacuees until their re-evacuation in 1940 and was very honoured to receive the certificate from the Queen.

I WISH TO MARK, BY THIS PERSONAL MESSAGE, my appreciation of the service you have rendered to your Country in 1939.

In the early days of the War you opened your door to strangers who were in need of shelter, & offered to share your home with them.

I know that to this unselfish task you have sacrificed much of your own comfort, & that it could not have been achieved without the loyal co-operation of all in your household.

By your sympathy you have earned the gratitude of those to whom you have shown hospitality, & by your readiness to serve you have helped the State in a work of great value.

Mrs. Ruffle.

"There was a huge crater, so deep that the bomb had made no sound."

Mrs Betty Taylor, Maldon, Essex - compiled from a letter and interview

Mrs Betty Taylor and her husband Eric McClelland Taylor, who was the sanitary inspector and meat inspector with Maldon Borough Council, were living at 23 Washington Road when war broke out:

After the raids began, some schools were evacuated to "safe" areas, and billeting officers called on inhabitants in order to ascertain the number of vacant bedrooms and later to allocate evacuees.

I felt that I could cope with a little girl, but when "Pip" Downes, one of my grammar school masters, turned up with two young men taller than myself, I was rather taken aback!

The boys were from Wanstead County High School, and one, Eric Hutchins, returned home after three weeks.

He was rather an introverted type of boy and though I tried hard to make his time with us as happy as possible, I could not establish any kind of rapport.

The other, Donald Hunt, was an extrovert and charming, obviously from a different background from Eric, but they were great friends.

Donald went home at weekends occasionally and on returning, he asked my permission to bring his accordion. What pleasure we had from those sessions and whenever I hear "The Blue Danube" or "Skaters Waltz" I think of Donald. He also played the clarinet in the excellent school orchestra.

Rationing was a problem – 2 ozs butter, 2 ozs margarine, etc. etc., per person and growing boys have large appetites, but we shared whatever was available and everyone seemed to be satisfied. We were allowed eight shillings and sixpence per week for each evacuee, but in Donald's case, his parents sent the same weekly amount.

I was sorry when they all moved to other areas, as I grew attached to Donald and have never heard of either boy again, though occasionally I have read notices of an organ recital to be given by Donald Hunt and wondered if he could be my evacuee.

I remember a battle being fought above the school field one Saturday afternoon when a cricket match was being played. Rumour had it that a man who kept a small nursery garden in The Chase near the Conservative Club, ran up and down his garden in order to avoid the firing, shouting "I'll fool the ....s!"

Several planes were brought down, one at Langford I believe and after the all-clear people walked there in droves to view the wreckage. By some means at a later date I acquired a Nazi medal and length of thick, green parachute card (possibly from a land mine).

I have very vivid memories of the night when a bomb fell in the small hours in Washington Road. It was a cloudy night and a sneak raider evaded search lights and the Observer Corps at their posts in grammar school field, during one of the nightly missions to London. So the information had not been circulated to the ARP (Air Raid Precautions) mobile unit centre where I did duty as a volunteer.

Though we had been provided with an indoor table shelter, (some people made their own dug-outs in their gardens). We were tired of so many nights of discomfort and on that particular night had risked going upstairs to bed.

In case of an emergency or incident I kept my uniform by my bed and was supposed to run when necessary to the units above the building which is now Quest Motors in the High Street.

I was awakened by a deafening roar, nudged my husband and we instinctively rolled out of bed on either side and underneath it, clasping our heads and awaiting the collapse of the roof. Instead there was an uncanny silence and at length we crawled out, hastily donned our clothes and emerged. The front door had burst open, there was plaster, etc. all down the stairs and when we reached our front gate we could not believe our eyes. Instead of the neat row of semi-detached houses, just beyond ours, there was a huge crater, so deep that the bomb had made no sound. The last house remained standing, but was sliced in half. We could hear cries for help under the rubble and were so shocked we had difficulty in remembering who occupied the houses, though we knew them all well.

I felt sure the mobile unit would be along in minutes, so began to give what assistance I could unaware that the alarm had not been raised. Fred Rath, the borough engineer joined us, bringing a ladder. He and my husband rescued several people, using doors which had been blown off, as stretchers, and made them as comfortable as possible by the side of the road. Neighbours ran out with blankets, cups of tea, etc. By this time another friend and volunteer, Gwen Boreham, had been assisting wherever possible – she and I were very worried at the non-arrival of the unit which would have brought Dr Cragg-Simpson, the MO (Medical Officer) and others. Hours seemed to pass before the unit arrived, the officer in charge being Mr E M Williams, another of my grammar school masters. The WRVS came also, dispensing tea, but neighbours had surely used their weekly rations by this time. There were some miraculous escapes, but the digging went on for hours.

The last to be unearthed were Harry and Gertrude Wright, as they were under the rubble of their own and the next door house. Harry was an Air Raid Warden and we had always felt so "safe" in the black out, even from the enemy, when he was on duty walking in the road. His cheerful voice as he chatted to his fellow warden seemed to bring normality to us all in those dark days.

Now he and his wife whom I'd known most of my life were gone, also Stamford Card and family, Sid Joslin and wife and others, and it is true to say that I never fully recovered from the horrors of that night. I could not remain in the house at night if the siren sounded, but we would walk in the streets until the ALL CLEAR, as I had developed a horror of being buried under rubble.

At a later date a public meeting was held in St Peter's Hospital to discuss the incident, and I was both surprised and hurt when Gwen and I were

NAZI BOMBS KILL EIGHT PERSONS IN RESIDENTIAL TOWN

OTHERS IN REMARKABLE ESCAPES

By J. C. CHAPLIN

EARLY on Saturday one of the enemy air raiders which managed to cross our coast during the night dropped bombs on a residential district of a small coastal town. Eight people were killed and seven injured, two of them seriously. Fourteen houses were either wholly or partly demolished.

The casualties included the following people killed: Mr. and Mrs. H. C. Wright, Mr. John W. Dykes, Mr. and Mrs. Harold S. Joscelyne, Mr. and Mrs. Stanford C. Card, and their young son, Peter Stanford Card. Mr. Wright was an air raid warden, and his wife was a school teacher. They had packed up ready to go to London in the morning for the week-end. Mr. Joscelyne was a clerk in Maldon Post-office. His father was killed in the last war. Mr. Card was a 'bus driver. His wife's parents, Mr. and Mrs. Barrett, were living in another part of the town, having come there after having been bombed out in London. A district nurse lodging with Mr. and Mrs. Card received injuries to her thigh and back. Mrs. Judd was injured, and taken to St. Peter's Hospital.

The damage was confined to two roads, one leading off the other.

Most of the casualties occurred at the end of a road, where two blocks of semi-detached houses received a direct hit. In the other road, four houses were practically wrecked, but the residents had remarkable escapes. They were: Mr. and Mrs. E. D. Roberts, Mr. and Mrs. Barwell and their two daughters, Jean and Barbara, Mrs. Rees and her daughter, Iris, and Mr. and Mrs. J. Gower and their child Michael. Mrs. Rees had an injured knee and suffered from shock, but otherwise none received physical hurt.

SAVED BY HELMET

Mr. Roberts is 68, and a Special Constable. His wife is 72. He had come off reserve duty and heard a 'plane overhead. "That sounds like a German," he said to his wife. He still had his uniform on, and putting on his steel helmet, he went to the front door. There came a terrific crash. Although stunned he called to his wife to "take cover." More crashes followed. Mr. Roberts called to his wife, as debris flew in all directions, "For heaven's sake keep against the chimney."

"I rushed back into the sitting room and covered my face," Mr. Roberts told an ESSEX CHRONICLE reporter. "I think my life was saved by my helmet."

After seeing that his wife was uninjured Mr. Roberts went on duty, and, in the words of colleagues, he did excellent work, and remained on duty for several hours.

"He was a brick, with no thought of himself—only for his wife and others," said a police colleague afterwards.

BLOWN OUT OF BED

The Barwells, too, were very lucky people. Their house was the most damaged of all in this road. One of the daughters was blown out of bed, and in the place where she had been sleeping there crashed a piece of concrete weighing several hundredweight.

"She's a very fortunate girl," said Mr. Barwell, who is an income tax official at Witham. He, too, is a Special Constable. "Mind my flowers, old man," he said, as members of the rescue party came to the house.

Mrs. Rees, who was in bed at the time, was not quite so fortunate as the others. She was struck by falling debris, but her injuries are not serious.

Mr. and Mrs. Gower and Michael got out of their house—uninjured. "That was a near thing," said Mr. Gower, with

a wry smile, as he looked at his ruined home.

In the other road there was a scene of devastation. In one wrecked house rescue squads worked untiringly, and extricated Mr. and Mrs. G. F. Rose, and their eight-year-old daughter. They were uninjured, although Mrs. Rose, badly shocked, was taken to hospital. She was later discharged. Mr. Dykes, who lodged with Mr. and Mrs. Rose, was killed. He was over 70, and blind. Mr. Rose, who was dug out in his pyjamas, was for several hours pinned by part of a chimney stack. He is a salesman for Messrs. Markham, mineral water manufacturers.

Mr. and Mrs. Ward owe their lives to war work. They were on night work when their house was hit. Mr. Vyse, whose bungalow was wrecked, happened to be sleeping that night with his nephew, Mr. Bert Gowen.

FINE A.R.P. SERVICE.

The A.R.P. and other services worked splendidly. Many of the men worked 12 hours without a break except to have a cup of tea at the mobile canteen presented to the town by residents of the sister town in America This was the canteen's first serious "job," and it did it well. "I don't know what we should have done without it," said Mr. T. J. Howson Russell, who was in charge of the A.R.P. Members of the W.V.S., under Mrs. Blind, the Centre organiser, operated the canteen in a highly efficient manner. Men from a Bomb Disposal Squad did magnificent clearing up work.

The Mayor, Ald. S. G. Tydeman, J.P., lives only a hundred or so yards from the spot, but his house was undamaged.

The funeral of Mr. and Mrs. Card and their child was on Tuesday. Mr. Dykes was also buried on Tuesday. The funerals of Mr. and Mrs. Joscelyne and Mr. and Mrs. Wright were yesterday. The Mayor, members of the Corporation, and large numbers of townspeople attended the funerals.

During the last war a Zeppelin dropped bombs, mostly incendiaries, on this town, but there were no serious casualties.

Some persons were killed and others injured when houses were completely demolished and thi.. by bombs dropped on an East Coast town in the early hours of Saturday m

reprimanded for not reporting for duty, but going instead, straight to the area of devastation.

On the morning after the bomb Mrs Taylor invited a family in for breakfast who had been bombed out of their house at 35 Washington Road. They were George and Harriet Rose, the parents of a little girl called Vera Rose...

THE CHILDREN'S VIEW

"I would not let them play on my two wheeled bike because that was very special."

Interview with Mrs Vera Scott (Née Rose), Tollesbury, Essex

Vera was eight years old and living at 35 Washington Road, Maldon when Mrs Blind, head of the WVS, came to the house in the early evening with the billeting officer and two very bedraggled looking little girls. They had gas masks on their shoulders and cheap attaché cases, and one had a teddy bear. Mrs Blind asked her mother, Harriet Rose, to take the children as they were the last two and they couldn't find a home for them.

The little girls were Ruth and Gwen. Vera recalls that they came in the spring of 1940, so they were late arrivals which could explain the difficulty in finding a billet for them. They travelled to Maldon by train, arriving at Maldon East Station at the bottom of Market Hill. She recalls the girls had been eating biscuits and drinking bottles of 'pop' and when they arrived they didn't want any tea. As an only child she resented having two little girls in the house and when they went she was glad to have her own space back.

"I didn't want the girls to come. The house was brand new and had a real bathroom. We chose number 35. I thought the house was quite crowded already. We had three bedrooms and we shared the house with my aunt and an old man we called 'Granddad'. Because I was an only child I think I was a bit selfish in those days and I didn't want them playing with my toys, but mother said they were staying and that I must share my toys. I shared most of them but I would not let them play on my two wheeled bike because that was very special. I remember going with my father to buy it from Maldon Cycle Shop. It was a Royal Enfield with black handlebars and cost eight pounds and a shilling."

The girls came from two separate families and had never met before that day. Ruth came from Woodford Green and Vera believes Gwen came from a Dr Barnardos children's home. Gwen was very quiet and studious, but Ruth was a bit of a character.

"She was a 'little devil'. We all used to play together but it was Ruth who always had the ideas for games which got us all into trouble. She was the youngest but we still used to follow her. I remember a day when it was snowing and Ruth ploughed through the snow and we followed, and we all got told off. Washington Road was a dead-end in those days and beyond it were fields belonging to Mr Binder. We used to go over the fields and play by the pond, finding tadpoles in the water. The field reached up to West Station Railway. Ruth led us up the railway bank where we walked along the line. We got into trouble with the controller."

Ruth went occasionally to visit her mother and always came back with some illness like chickenpox. Once she came back with nits in her hair. The only cure was to shave her head. Other children from school teased her and called her "a boy". Luckily the rest of them didn't catch any of the various ailments which were inflicted on poor Ruth.

Vera went to All Saints School in Maldon and the girls went with her. When the school became overcrowded – there were only five classes in the school – Vera wondered why these strangers were there. She didn't really understand what the evacuation was all about. However, when it was decided that they should split the day between the two groups of children, she was very pleased there would only be a half day at school.

The girls stayed just over a year until 1941. Ruth came back to visit when she was 18 or 19 and married, but they never heard anything from Gwen.

Later in the war Maldon was considered to be a possible landing place for the Germans, so 'dragons teeth' and concrete blocks were built around the promenade to stop the tanks coming through. There never was a land invasion on the Essex coast but Vera remembers the German planes coming over Maldon.

"Sometimes we saw German pilots flying overhead taking photos. On one occasion I was with several children picking blackberries and out of the blue a German plane came over and swooped down low. We all jumped into the ditch and lost all the blackberries. He machine-gunned the fields next to us. We were terrified. Afterwards we picked up shells and kept them. I still have mine."

Her father wasn't called up because he was partially deaf so he joined the Home Guard. He spent a lot of time "out on manoeuvres". The shed in their garden was requisitioned to hold bombs and hand grenades for the Home Guard. Vera recalls sitting in the shed with an illicit cigarette made from her dad's tobacco papers and dried apple leaves, surrounded by all the ammunition!

Exactly a year after the evacuees left, in the early hours of the morning on 30th May 1942, the family were bombed out of 35 Washington Road. Eight people died that night. Both families next door were killed, so was the old man who was living with them and her aunt.

"The house was totally destroyed but I and my mother and father survived. There was no warning siren on the night of the bomb. A German aircraft was separated from the others and was being followed by search lights. To hasten his departure he dropped his load, others went off in Fambridge Road."

"I woke up to find myself hanging from the bedstead. It seemed like I hung there for hours. When they got me down I only had a cut on my leg but they took me to St Peter's Hospital. The next day I remember that Matron Tait said 'I have a surprise for you'. I thought the surprise would be some sort of present, but the surprise was my father who was there to visit me. I only had my

VERA ROSE'S MONKEY

RED HAT AND LONG TAIL AND LOOKING RATHER BATTERED

By JUNELLA CHAPPELLE

SEVEN-year-old Vera Rose went to bed early last Friday evening in a quiet little house which stood in a rather insignificant little street in a quiet little East Anglian town. A few hours later a German 'plane flew low over the town and released four bombs. One fell on the house where Vera Rose was sleeping.

Where her house stood there is now a large crater, and the houses next door but one, two, and three have gone too. I found Vera's brown toy monkey when I climbed over the great clods of earth and brickwork which surround the crater. The monkey was very battered, and had a red hat and a long tail. I wanted to take it along to Vera Rose, who is now in hospital, for it looked as though it might be mighty important to her; but the policeman on duty would not let me take it away from the scene, so I left it in his care for Vera Rose. She was not hurt very much, mainly shock.

Her father and mother were with her in hospital at first, but her father has since been discharged. One of the rescue party told me that when Mr. Rose was found beneath some protecting rafters he sat up in bed stretched, and said, "How do you do, Mr. So-and-So!"

"I'M HERE, I'M HERE"

The rescue party heard shouts coming from an old lady somewhere in the crater. They searched along the sides of the crater in vain, and still the voice kept crying, "I'm here, I'm here." They found her at last, in bed, perched on top of the ruins of her home.

Another man and his wife were not so fortunate. Living in the house at one end of the four which were hit, they were found against the bedroom wall, which was all that remained of the further end house.

Mr. W. F. Sherrington, who lives opposite to the house where Vera Rose used to live, said to me:

"My wife and I had only just gone to bed. We had been to a neighbour's house-warming party, and I don't think any of us will ever forget that house-warming. I heard the 'plane come over, and thought it must be a Jerry. Then I heard another 'plane, which was unmistakably one of our fighters. After that there came a burst of cannon fire, and I thought, 'He'll start unloading now,' and he did. We tumbled out on the floor, just as we heard the whistle of the bomb. There seemed to be a terrific concentrated crunch, and the acrid smell which we used to call cordite, which always follows an explosion, filled the room. I did not think it was so near.

"I fell into what pieces of my special police uniform which were handy, and ran to the telephone. The front door was wide open, and just as I picked up the telephone, to find it dead, the man at whose home we had had been all the evening came up the path and said that half the houses opposite were down. The first thing we heard was a rather terrible moaning from the far side of the crater, where half a house was standing. We could see into the bedrooms, because it was brilliant moonlight, and the moaning seemed to be coming from one of those.

DOUBLE CHAIN OF MEN

"The builders have not long finished building our house, and I knew where they had left a long ladder. I ran to fetch it, and propped it up against the wall. It was a long ladder, and sloped a great deal towards the crater. By that time the first-aid party were on the scene. I went up first, and Miss Metcalfe, of the F.A.P., came after me. We found the two people who had been blasted from the other house in that room. They were still alive. The rescue squad got them out and on to stretchers. Then the rest of the men formed a double chain all along the brink of the crater, and handed the stretchers from pair to pair to the road.

"The crater was much deeper then, at the beginning, than it is now, and one false step in the dark would have sent them right to the bottom; but nobody thought of themselves that night at all. There was none of the 'Why should I take orders from you?' sort of thing which is common to practices and exercises between A.R.P. and police personnel. Everyone did what he was told, providing it was a sensible thing to do (and there were no foolish orders), never minding who told him."

The bomb went deep into the ground, and then exploded upwards, so that the blast went fanwise. A greenhouse in a garden behind the crater had two panes of glass out, caused by falling bricks, while houses many yards away had their windows blown in.

THE CHEERFUL KETTLE

On top of the pile at one side of the crater I saw the sun glinting on something. I went closer, to see what it was. It was a chromium kettle, resting on top of the bricks, its spout pointing cheerfully skywards, and not a dent in its plating. A child's fairy cycle hung, twisted and bent, from a broken wall, where it had landed. There were peas and potatoes coming along very well in the gardens of the houses that are no longer there. I found a pepper box in the rockery garden, and there were tins of beans peeping beneath the bricks.

One man who lost his home is alive to-day because he was fire-watching. By a freak of fate his wife went with him for company. If their son had been home on leave for the week-end, as he often was, before he was sent abroad, they would both have been at home.

Four more houses were wrecked in a nearby road. Two bombs exploded in the front gardens of these. I was told a story about a man who lived in one of them, who, after crawling out himself and getting his wife out, went around to the kitchen at the back, and accidentally touched the electric switch. The light came on. Then he and his wife went to relatives further down the road, and found them sitting in the dark. "The lights have gone," they explained. "Then let's go back to my house. Our lights are on," he said.

A recently-married couple with new furniture, living in a nearby house, dived on to the floor when they heard the 'plane coming over, and there made the discovery that modern beds are not made to get under.

WAS IT A STUKA?

In these houses the casualties were a bruised thigh and a bruised knee. In the first road, eight were killed and four injured. People who saw the 'plane caught in the searchlights say it was a Stuka dive-bomber, and it is believed to have been brought down further along the coast by a pilot from a nearby aerodrome.

From the A.R.P. point of view everything went with the precision of a practise. The parties were on the spot in a matter of seconds, and were relieved in order. One man, Rescue Party Leader Clark, refused to go home, and was on duty for sixteen hours till the last body was recovered. One slightly unhappy turn of phrase gave me a minor shock when I was told at the control office, "We sent some men to dig out the manageress of the British Restaurant to cook breakfast for the Civil Defence workers at seven o'clock."

The tea car, which was only recently presented to the town by its namesake in America, was also promptly on the spot, and was greatly appreciated. There is nothing like a cup of tea to soothe the dust-caked throats of the rescue squads.

As I stood looking down into the crater, fifteen 'planes went over, flying low, and their shadows flashed for a second across the wreckage. Looking up, I could see the red, white, and blue rings on their wings, and they looked good and avenging to me as they flew out to sea. This was the first time in this war that anybody has been killed by a bomb in the quiet little town. Many individual acts of what we would call bravery were done that night; but the people who did them would hate to be called heroes.

WHEN WILL IT END?

nightdress and people in the district gave me things to wear including a lovely blue dress. Everyone pointed me out in the town which was very embarrassing. Flocks of people came up the road to look at the bomb crater."

The family lost everything, even Vera's precious two wheeled bike and the piano. When war damage money was paid out people got paid for furniture but not luxury items. Vera used to play the piano and she gave her first recital in the infant class wearing an old dress of her mother's. But because the piano was considered a luxury item it wasn't replaced, so later she took up violin and played 2nd violin in Maldon orchestra.

On Friday 5th June 1942 the Essex Chronicle published an article about the bomb, which described the incident as, "the first time in the war that anybody had been killed by a bomb in a quiet little town". There was also an article entitled, "Vera Rose's Monkey" in which the journalist claims to have found a toy monkey with a red hat belonging to Vera, which she tried to deliver (unsuccessfully) to the hospital where Vera stayed that night. Vera was quite indignant about the story because she didn't own the monkey, (she felt she was too old for that sort of toy). It belonged to the little boy who lived next door but one, Peter Card, who was tragically killed in the blast with his parents, at the tender age of three.

"We were 'country bumpkins' but they were 'townies'"
Interview with Mr Alec Cornwell, Witham, Essex

Alec is a Maldonian who lived in a cottage near the Queen Victoria pub in Spital Road, Maldon, during the war. He went to school with the evacuee boys at the Council Senior School in Wantz Road.

He knew Jean and Peter Torrance, who lodged with farmer John Brown and others who were billeted with Mr Gibbons, headmaster of Heybridge School. Although he didn't mind the evacuees being there he felt that the local children and the newcomers didn't have much in common.

"We were 'country bumpkins' but they were 'townies'. There was a bit of teasing going on. Mr Hornet, the headmaster of the Secondary School, got everything pretty much back to normal after the evacuees arrived. We had sticky paper blackouts on the windows and shelters in the corridors."

Alec remembers that Maldon had its share of enemy action. One of his teachers was killed in Washington Road when it was bombed. He also has a first hand memory of the day the school was machine-gunned.

"A German aeroplane came over and shot at the school. We heard the siren going and went into the corridor shelters. There were used bullet cases in the school playground which we collected later."

He also tells some rather frightening stories of boyish pranks during the war.

"One time we found incendiary bombs in the Leper Colony. We threw them at the walls to make them go off. On another occasion the Germans dropped a land mine down near the cemetery. I remember two boys trying to chisel nuts off. One of those boys later became a policeman!"

"When the doodlebugs started coming over one dropped nearby and blew the roof off our house. The tiles fell on me in the air raid shelter."

Alec recalls there were a lot of troops in the district, including the Argyle and Southern Highlanders. He also met the "Land Girls".

"They were at Spital Farm, which belonged to Mr Binder. They were good workers and commanded respect. One could lift a two and a half hundred-weight sack of corn, and all the women used thrashing tackle. I used to work for Mr Binder on a milk round and would much rather be there than at school. Charlie Binder was very strong. As his party trick a lady called Reene Price used to stand on his shovel and he would lift her up. I didn't meet any conscientious objectors but I knew they worked for the timber merchants cutting wood."

Alec remembers the area becoming a restricted or "banned" zone.

"Police stopped the buses coming into the district along the Woodham Mortimer main road and anyone who had no business here was turned away."

Alec left school in 1943, stayed in Maldon until he was called up in 1947 to join the Army. He came back in 1949 after being in Egypt.

The following extract from the Civil Defence War Diary shows just how dangerous the "game" of playing with unexploded bombs could be:

DATE.	TIME.	PLACE.	MISSILE.
15/7/41.	14.45.	Pea Field, Grange Farm, Cold Norton.	2" Trench Mortar Shell.
CASUALTIES.		REMARKS.	
4 injured – 1 serious		Children were examining the shell when it exploded.	

THE ONE WHO GOT AWAY

With the growing threat of invasion new ways were found to evacuate children. Some were sent abroad as far afield as Canada and Australia. Long after all the other letters came in an airmail letter arrived from an evacuee who had been sent from Maldon to South Africa.

"Send my greetings to my Maldon birth place."

Letter from Barbara Browne (Née Turner), Cape Town, South Africa

I happened to purchase some out of date magazines at an R15 a kilo outlet – 2lbs 2oz for only £2.50!! Amongst my choices was "Yours" Spring Special 1995 with your letter to the editor.

I was born in Maldon, Essex in 1924 and went to Mrs Knowles' (long closed down) private school in Cromwell Hill – we were living in the White House in Silver Street 1925 - 1932 or 3 and then moved to Fambridge Road which my father had built – £1,000, plot included! My father, Thomas Turner, was a maths and Latin master at the (then) Maldon Grammar School under Mr Deedes' and later Mr Ince's headmasterships and took Cambridge School Leaving Certificate in July 1940 – under threat of bombings and even Nazi invasion!

In 1939 my father was an evacuation officer for Wanstead High School which was evacuated to Maldon, and who used the grammar school premises in the afternoons – with their teachers. He roped me in to help – in the area near the "Prom" – a council estate – I can't recall its name. We had two soldiers billeted with us – their heavy boots "wore out" the new stair carpets, much to my mother's chagrin!

My sister, Betty and I, then aged 14 and 15 respectively, were evacuated by ship to Cape Town, leaving Liverpool in August '40 and arriving here in September. I was engaged by the end of the war to a South African of Irish parents, who had volunteered (all SAs were volunteers) and allowed to stay on and not return to England with the other evacuees.

I have been back – but could never settle after this South African experience – in fact 55 years now!

Send my greetings to my Maldon birth place.

Children embarking at a British port to be evacuated to Austraila, 19 August 1940.

Photograph – Imperial War Museum

STOP PRESS. . .STOP PRESS. . .STOP PRESS. . .

As this book was going to press I received the following letter from Mrs Doris Martin of Hainault, Essex:

I have been given a copy of "Essex Countryside" and read your letter. Although the following story might not be the information you are looking for I thought you might be interested to read it.

I worked with Ivy Barritt before the war and we became good friends. I thought she was the most angelic person I had ever known, a dear one. She told me that whilst on a convalescent trip at Maldon she met Stanford. He was well known at the local C of E church and a bell ringer there.

They married before the war and settled in a new house in Maldon and were so happy together. I was able to visit them and to know their little boy Peter, a loveable child.

During the war Ivy invited me to stay, it meant getting a "permit" to travel. Before I could get the permit Ivy's twin sister contacted me to tell me the sad news that Ivy, Stanford and their dear little Peter, three years old, had been killed. A German plane jettisoned its bombs over Maldon and their house was demolished. They were found over Peter's cot as if trying to shield him.

I understand a nurse staying with them was badly injured.

Ivy was Roy Whiteman's aunt, who lived in Washingtom Road, and little Peter was the owner of the monkey with the red hat.

POSTSCRIPT

In the course of compiling this book, many questions were raised about people, places times and dates.

If you are someone of whom one of the contributors to this book has said, "I wonder where they are now", and would like to get in touch, please write to me and I will pass on your contact details. The address to write to is:-

Migration to Maldon
Maldon District Council
Princes Road
Maldon
Essex
CM9 5DL

This book is published by Maldon District Council in commemoration of all those who lived through World War II, in the hope that there will never again be a need to send children away from home in an evacuation scheme.

APPENDIX

SOME BACKGROUND TO MALDON DISTRICT

Maldon District is on the east coast of Essex, less than 50 miles from the centre of London. Today's visitors would find many parts of Maldon District little changed since the war years. It is still possible to visit the remains of St Giles Leper Hospital in Maldon, the Chapel of St Peter-on-the-Wall at Bradwell, the Plume Library and Moot Hall at Maldon, The Quay at Burnham-on-Crouch, and many other places mentioned in these reminiscences. Promenade Park, with its Marine Lake, has changed little since Victorian times and is still very much at the heart of the town.

Maldon is one of the two oldest towns in Essex. The name Maldon derives from the Anglo-Saxon for a cross on a hill top, and a burh (fort) was built here by King Edward the Elder in 916 to defend the river Blackwater against the Norsemen. The famous "Battle of Maldon" took place here in 991, when the Saxon Earl Bryhtnoth led the battle against the Viking invaders but was defeated; the story is depicted in the earliest recorded Saxon epic poem. Maldon District has a rich maritime heritage dating back to pre-Roman times. The picturesque Thames sailing barges are still based at Hythe Quay in Maldon. They were once used as working barges but now are used mainly for recreation.

Burnham-on-Crouch on the River Crouch, is believed to date from 1253 when a market charter was granted to the Fitzwalter family. It became very popular as a yachting centre in the 19th century and is still a successful resort today; known as "The Cowes of the East Coast".

Maldon District is very much part of "real" Essex and is perhaps its best kept secret. The district has many miles of coast, saltmarshes, rare plants and wildlife, large conservation areas and historic churches. The villages in the district such as Tillingham, Bradwell-on-Sea, Tolleshunt D'Arcy and Tollesbury still retain much of their "old world" charm.

For more information about places to visit in the district please contact Maldon Tourist Information Centre, Coach Lane Maldon, Essex or telephone 01621 856503. The centre is open Monday - Saturday 10.00am - 4.00pm. (Saturdays in winter 10.00am - 1.30pm.)

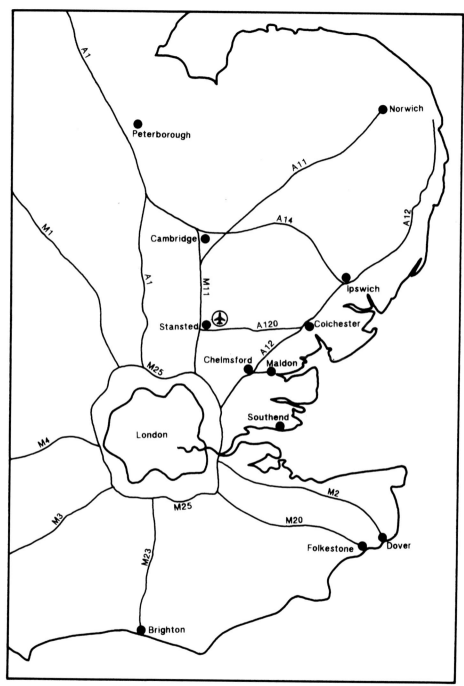

Maldon District is on the east coast of England

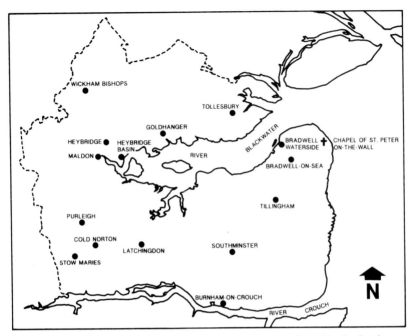

Maldon District – showing towns and villages mentioned in the book.

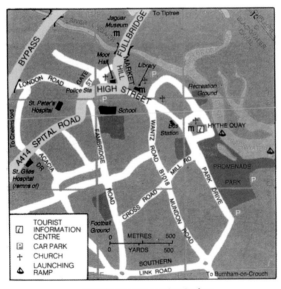

Maldon town centre today

Charles Grig Tait's 1939 drawing of Maldon High Street. Except for the changes in the names of the shops it looks very much the same today.

8th June, 1946

To-day, as we celebrate victory, I send this personal message to you and all other boys and girls at school. For you have shared in the hardships and dangers of a total war and you have shared no less in the triumph of the Allied Nations.

I know you will always feel proud to belong to a country which was capable of such supreme effort; proud, too, of parents and elder brothers and sisters who by their courage, endurance and enterprise brought victory. May these qualities be yours as you grow up and join in the common effort to establish among the nations of the world unity and peace.

George R.I.